One Sure Thing

The Power Of A Life Grounded In Assurance

by Robert Harman

First Book in the Life-Planted Discipleship Series for personal and group Bible study

"that you, being rooted and grounded..."
Ephesians 3:17

Endorsements

"*One Sure Thing* is a must-have addition for any believer who wants to confidently 'handle the word of truth.' I am excited to see this foundational material being made available."

- Dr. Eric Scalise, CEO of Alignment Association, former VP of the American Association of Christian Counselors, and former Dept. Chair for Counseling Programs at Regent University

"*One Sure Thing* is a definitive resource, a must! It should be provided to all so that they may be firmly grounded in the faith."

- The Very Rev. Ralph L. Frye, Canon (ret.), Convocation of Anglicans in North America (CANA), Mission of the Anglican Church of Nigeria

"...a fascinating study of practical Christianity. It is meticulous!"

- Alex Lykhosherstov, PhD candidate, South African Theological Seminary, translator of the Russian edition

"The studies contained here changed my life, like nothing else before or since!"

- Bobby Farino, President, American Golf Classics

"For over four decades, the teachings of One Sure Thing have helped me grow in Christ. It is a faithful guide to biblical discipleship, and I pray that many others will likewise grow and thrive through this invaluable resource."

– Rev. James Beavers, Orange, Virginia

One Sure Thing

Copyright ©2016 by Robert Harman. All rights reserved. No portion of this book may be reproduced, stored in a retrieval system, or transmitted in any form except for brief quotations in printed reviews, without the prior permission of the publisher.

Published by

Wellhouse Publishers

Williamsburg, Virginia 23185, USA

Book Design and Illustrations
by C. Michael Johnson

Scripture quotations unless otherwise marked are from the New American Standard Bible® (NASB), Copyright © 1960, 1962, 1963, 1968, 1971, 1972, 1973, 1975, 1977, 1995 by The Lockman Foundation. Used by permission. www.Lockman.org

Scripture quotations marked (NIV) are taken from the Holy Bible, New International Version®, NIV®. Copyright © 1973, 1978, 1984, 2011 by Biblica, Inc.™ Used by permission of Zondervan. All rights reserved worldwide. www.zondervan.com The "NIV" and "New International Version" are trademarks registered in the United States Patent and Trademark Office by Biblica, Inc.™

About the Author

Robert Harman has been teaching the Bible for over forty years and is passionate about seeing people established in their faith. He has taught this material in many places of the world, including Ukraine, Russia, Armenia, Nepal, Japan, Trinidad and Europe. It was previously published in Russian and 5000 copies distributed, but this is the first time it is available in English. A science major and graduate of William & Mary, he was a policeman for 26 years and a campus minister and pastor for 15. He and his wife, Johanna, live in Williamsburg, Virginia. They have two daughters and two adorable grandsons.

"My goal as you read is revelation — that God would speak to your heart and make His truth unshakeable in you."

I have created this book with you, the reader, in mind. From the beginning the lessons were created and used for a small group setting and nothing would please me more than to assist you in teaching these lessons to others. To that end, student notes are available, FREE, that you can download and print for your study group as 8.5 x 11 worksheets. Just visit my website, **RobertharmanAuthor.com** for these and other free resources. You can also contact me there. I pray this book and the added resources will bring a rich, transformational experience in your pursuit of finding this hugely important 'one sure thing.'

Be truly blessed!

Robert

FREE DOWNLOAD

Student Notes

Get a free download of the complete set of Student Notes, study guides and extras at
RobertHarmanAuthor.com

Write the Author at:
Bob@RobertHarmanAuthor.com

For Johanna

My best fan and most valued critic,

each year together

makes me even more appreciative

of how awesome you are.

Table of Contents

Chapter 1	Who Do You Say Jesus Is?	11
Chapter 2	The Man Christ Jesus	27
Chapter 3	Why Jesus Came	39
Chapter 4	Justified by Faith	47
Chapter 5	The Three Parts of Salvation	55
Chapter 6	Repentance	67
Chapter 7	Faith	81
Chapter 8	Water Baptism	89
Chapter 9	The Baptism in the Holy Spirit	99
Chapter 10	Resurrections of the Dead	113
Chapter 11	Believers' Judgment of Rewards	123
Chapter 12	Eternal Judgment of the Lost	135
Chapter 13	Jesus' Suffering in Hell	145
Chapter 14	Eternal Security	157
Chapter 15	Questions about Eternal Security	165
Chapter 16	The New Covenant	173
Appendixes		183

    A Is Water Baptism Essential for Salvation?
    B Schools of Thought concerning the Millennium
    C The Unforgivable Sin
    D Calvinism and Arminianism
    E Predestined to What?

Chapter One
Who Do You Say Jesus Is?

Speculation about Jesus' Identity

He wrote no book, yet more books have been written about him than any person in history. He composed no music, but more music has been composed about him than anyone else. Even though his life was cut off in its prime, it impacted history as no other and his biography has been translated into more languages than any other. Only twelve enrolled in his "school," yet today more than a billion people consider themselves to be his followers. I'm referring, of course, to Jesus of Nazareth. Who was this person, Jesus?

As we read the New Testament 2000 years after Jesus walked the earth, and especially because many of us have heard the stories about Jesus since childhood, it's easy for us to miss the whirl of speculation that was in the air at that time, about who this person might be. Imagine hearing about Him for the first time! Huge crowds flock to a man whose teachings are powerful and whose works are miraculous. In town after town he heals the sick, and there are reports that he even makes blind people see and lame people walk. Speculation about his identity swirls around him as everyone from kings to common folks try to figure out who he is. Everyone has their own opinion: some say He is Elijah or another Old Testament prophet who has come back from the dead. Others brand Him a false prophet who leads people astray or is demon-possessed! At the same time, many wonder if this could be the long-awaited Messiah, the deliverer who would lead Israel to recover its lost greatness.

As you read the first three quotations, notice not only the questions being asked, but who is doing the asking.

> *Luke 9:7-9 Now Herod the tetrarch heard of all that was happening; and he was greatly perplexed, because it was said by some that John had risen from the dead, and by some that Elijah had appeared, and by others, that one of the prophets of old had risen again. And Herod said, "I myself had John beheaded; but who is this man about whom I hear such things?" And he kept trying to see Him.*

> *Matthew 21:8-11 And most of the multitude spread their garments in the road, and others were cutting branches from the trees, and spreading them in the road. And the multitudes going before Him, and those who followed after were crying out, saying, "Hosanna to the Son of David; BLESSED IS HE WHO COMES IN THE NAME OF THE LORD; Hosanna in the highest!" And when He had entered Jerusalem, all the city was stirred, saying, "Who is this?" And the multitudes were saying, "This is the prophet Jesus, from Nazareth in Galilee."*

> *Mark 4:37-41 And there arose a fierce gale of wind, and the waves were breaking over the boat so much that the*

boat was already filling up. And He Himself was in the stern, asleep on the cushion; and they awoke Him and said to Him, "Teacher, do You not care that we are perishing?" And being aroused, He rebuked the wind and said to the sea, "Hush, be still." And the wind died down and it became perfectly calm. And He said to them, "Why are you so timid? How is it that you have no faith?" And they became very much afraid and said to one another, "Who then is this, that even the wind and the sea obey Him?"

In the first quote, Herod the king is puzzling over Jesus' identity. Next we read of the whole population of Jerusalem asking "Who is this?" And our last quote shows that at first, even the disciples did not know who Jesus was. They knew he was a Rabbi --a teacher-- with words unlike any they had ever heard and who was worth following. But it took some time before they discovered his true identity.

Let's take a quick tour through the 7th chapter of John to observe the heated-ness of the debate about Jesus. (verse 12) "There

was much grumbling among the crowds concerning Him; some were saying, 'He is a good man'; others were saying, 'No, on the contrary, He leads the people astray.' ...(verse 20) The crowd answered, 'You have a demon!' ...(verses 31-32) But many in the crowd believed in Him; and they were saying, 'When the Christ comes, He will not perform more signs than those which this man has, will He?' The Pharisees heard the crowd muttering these things about Him, and the chief priests and the Pharisees sent officers to seize Him. ...(verses 40-41) Some of the people therefore, when they heard these words, were saying, 'This certainly is the Prophet.' Others were saying, 'This is the Christ.' Still others were saying, 'Surely the Christ is not going to come from Galilee, is He?'"

Jesus' "Greater than" Statements

As the disciples were in the process of discovering who this man was, I'm sure they would have puzzled over his "greater than" statements. When understood in their historical context, these are simply awesome claims.

Matthew 12:41-42 The men of Nineveh will stand up with

Greater than...

Jonah	Solomon	The Temple
A Prophet	Wisest Man	Where Heaven meets earth

this generation at the judgment, and will condemn it because they repented at the preaching of Jonah; and behold, something greater than Jonah is here. The Queen of the South will rise up with this generation at the judgment and will condemn it, because she came from the ends of the earth to hear the wisdom of Solomon, and behold, something greater than Solomon is here.

Jesus claims to be greater than Jonah and greater than Solomon –

more than a prophet and more than a king. Now, Jonah was not the greatest of the prophets – that would have to be reserved for an Elijah or Isaiah. But Jonah was the greatest prophet in the "sign" he did. You'll remember that different prophets were given signs to perform, which acted out God's message for the people: cutting their hair and scattering it to the wind, for instance. But the "sign of Jonah" outshown any of these by a wide margin: he spent three days inside a whale and then came back from there! By saying that he is greater than Jonah, Jesus is saying that he is more than a prophet, and will perform a sign greater than Jonah's.

Jesus' claim to be greater than Solomon needs to be seen in light of what God said to Solomon in 1 Kings 3:12 "Behold, I have given you a wise and discerning heart, so that there has been no one like you before you, nor shall one like you arise after you." 1 Kings 4:29-33 describes Solomon's wisdom, "Now God gave Solomon wisdom and very great discernment and breadth of mind, like the sand on the seashore. Solomon's wisdom surpassed the wisdom of all the sons of the east and all the wisdom of Egypt. For he was wiser than all men." God made him wiser than any person in any generation, yet Jesus says that something greater than Solomon is with them!

The third "greater than" statement would have been even more astonishing to the Jewish ears that heard it:

Matthew 12:6 But I say to you that something greater than
the temple is here.

God promised Abraham to give him a land and be with him there. God instructed Moses to build a portable tabernacle in which He could dwell. And finally Solomon was permitted to build a permanent structure for God's presence. Thus we see the promise of a place to meet with God narrowing with the passage of the years to one point on the globe. For the Jews, the Temple embodied the right place to meet with God; the Torah (Law) the right way to meet with God. In the Temple, worship could be offered, help sought, forgiveness found. If you wanted to meet with God, you knew where to go to do it! And now Jesus was saying that they have something greater than the Temple with them!

> "His solemn and often-repeated warnings about the fate of Jerusalem in general and the Temple in particular raised the question not only of who he thought he was to pronounce such judgment (a prophet? the Messiah?) but also of what he thought YHWH would put in its place? ... We must remind ourselves, crucially, that the Temple was, after all, the central 'incarnational' symbol of Judaism. It was standard Jewish belief, rooted in Scripture and celebrated in regular festivals and liturgy, that the Temple was the place where heaven and earth actually interlocked, where the living God had promised to be present with his people. ...For Jesus to upstage the Temple, to take on its role and function...meant that Jesus was claiming that he rather than the Temple was the place where and the means by which the living God was present with Israel." (N.T. Wright, *The Challenge of Jesus*, IVP 1999, pp. 110-113.)

Greater than a prophet, greater than the wisest king, greater than the Temple – who was this man?

Peter's Realization

One day Jesus brought up this subject with His disciples. He began by asking who people said He was. They answered that people said many things. Matthew 16:13-14 "He began asking His disciples, saying, 'Who do people say that the Son of Man is?' And they said, 'Some say John the Baptist; and others, Elijah; but still others, Jeremiah, or one of the prophets.'"

But then Jesus asked what may be the most important question in the world.

> *Matthew 16:15-17 He said to them, "But who do you say that I am?" And Simon Peter answered and said, "Thou art the Christ, the Son of the living God." And Jesus answered and said to him, "Blessed are you, Simon Barjona, because flesh and blood did not reveal this to you, but My Father who is in heaven."*

To Jesus' question, "Who do you say that I am?" Peter answered, "You are the Christ," [the Greek translation of the Hebrew 'Messiah' or 'Anointed One'] "the Son of the living God." And did Jesus correct Peter, or commend him? He commended Peter's answer as the right answer, in fact an inspired answer.

As the passage continues, Jesus changes Peter's name from Simon ['sandy'] to Peter ['rock']. By doing this, Jesus was intimating that Peter would be transformed from someone as changeable as shifting sand into someone with stability: Matthew 16:18 "And I also say to you that you are Peter [Greek *petros*: a rock, a stone], and upon this rock [Gr. *petra*: bedrock] I will build My church." It's important that we recognize what Jesus is not saying here. Jesus is not saying the church would be built on Peter. It's unfortunate that we miss the distinction in English: Peter is a *petros*, a stone or pebble, but the Church would be built on *petra*, bedrock; the Church is built not on a stone but on bedrock. What is the *petra*, the bedrock, upon which the Church is built? It's the same revelation Peter received, that Jesus is God! No human ("flesh and blood") revealed it to Peter, but He received this knowledge as a revelation from God the Father. And I believe it's the same today: before we can see who Jesus is, the Father has to take away our spiritual blindness. Men and women may teach us, but God has to touch our understanding before it can become real to us.

The Bible clearly states that Jesus Christ is more than just a good man or one of the prophets. The Bible states that Jesus is God! Consider the following underlined phrases.

> *Titus 2:13 the glory of <u>our great God</u> and Savior, Christ Jesus.*
>
> *Hebrews 1:8 But <u>of the Son</u> He says, "Thy throne, <u>O God</u>, is forever and ever..."*
>
> *John 1:1, 14 In the beginning was the Word, and the Word was with God, and the Word <u>was God</u>. ...And the Word became flesh and dwelt among us.* [A]

What Jesus Said About His Identity

Let's look next at the words of Jesus Himself. Did Jesus ever directly tell people that He was God? Is it something people have made up about Him, or did He Himself make this claim?

> *John 8:56-59 Your father Abraham rejoiced to see my day, and he saw it, and was glad. The Jews therefore said to Him, "You are not yet fifty years old, and have you seen Abraham?"* [Jesus had just implied that He existed when Abraham lived.] *Jesus said to them, "Truly, truly, before Abraham was born, I am."*

In the Old Testament, the name of God used much more than any other is "*Yahweh*," sometimes written as "Jehovah." For some reason, in the King James Version and carrying into our modern translations this name is written "LORD" in capital letters (see footnote **B** for a brief explanation of how this came to be). *Yahweh* was the name revealed to Moses at the burning bush (Exodus 3:14), it occurs 6800 times in the Old Testament, and literally means, "I am."

So when Jesus said, "Before Abraham was, I am," He was not only claiming to have existed before Abraham, but he was using this most-revered name of God and applying it to Himself! If we would read "I am" every time our Old Testament has "LORD", we would get the full impact of Jesus' words in John 8: Jesus used God's name in the Old Testament as His own!

What about the people who heard Jesus say these words? Did they understand what He had just said? Did they realize that He had taken God's name for Himself? They certainly did! They picked up stones to kill Him for blasphemy!

It was obviously dangerous in that culture to openly announce you were God, so Jesus was selective when He did. Another time He plainly stated so is recorded in Luke 22.

> *Luke 22:66-71 And when it was day, the Council of elders of the people assembled, both chief priests and scribes, and they led Him away to their council chamber, saying, "If You are the Christ, tell us." But He said to them, "If I tell you, you will not believe; and if I ask a question, you will not answer. But from now on THE SON OF MAN WILL BE SEATED AT THE RIGHT HAND of the power OF GOD." And they all said, "Are You the Son of God, then?" And He said to them, "Yes, I am." And they said, "What further need do we have of testimony? For we have heard it ourselves from His own mouth."*

Jesus told His Jewish judges that He is the Son of God, and the judges had the same reaction as the crowd in John 8. They accused him of blasphemy – speech that mocks or shows contempt for God. In other words, for anyone who is not God to say, "I am God," it is mocking God! In this instance Jesus again clearly stated that He is God.

As an aside, this crime of blasphemy would not work in front of the Roman governor Pilate, because the Romans did not care about Jewish laws. So what crime could his accusers use to take Him to the Roman court? It seems that the Jewish judges, the Sanhedrin, are unprepared for this challenge; they stumble over themselves at first, saying that if he were not a criminal, they would not have brought Him

(John 18:30). That's equivalent to saying that everyone the police arrest must be guilty or they wouldn't be under arrest! How lame this was as a response was obvious to Pilate and it wouldn't pass the test of Roman justice, so next the Elders said Jesus was stirring up the nation and causing trouble (Luke 23:2, 5, 14) – He's a troublemaker. That still wasn't enough for Pilate -- after all, he had to have a specific crime that could be written on a placard and carried in front of the condemned man, then nailed to the cross above him. So next, Jesus' accusers said that He was claiming to be a king, and with this line of thought they found their trump card: anyone who claims to be a king is opposing Caesar -- and if you let Him go, Pilate, you are not a friend of Caesar (John 19:12)! This struck fear in Pilate's heart, who realized he could be in danger of being kicked out of the "friends of Caesar" club. This was an actual organization, very exclusive, with membership rings that had been presented to each person by Caesar himself. (As this part of the drama unfolds, I imagine Pilate twisting the ring on his finger.) Pilate's sense of political self-preservation was aroused and he condemned the man he did not want to condemn, writing Jesus' "crime" in this way: "Jesus of Nazareth, the King of the Jews" (John 19:19). Of course, having the crime phrased this way didn't thrill the Jewish leaders, who protested that a "he said" should be included: "he said he is King of the Jews." But by then Pilate was tired of their wrangling, and responded, "What I have written, I have written" (John 19:22).

Now let's continue with Jesus' claims. Here is another: John 10:30 "I and the Father are one" [literally "a unity", one nature]. The Hebrew of the Old Testament has two words for "one": *yacheed* means an absolute one while *echad* means a compound one, as in one cluster of grapes. When the oneness of God is written about, the word used is *echad*, for instance in Deuteronomy 6:4 "The LORD our God is one LORD."[c] So God is not a singularity of oneness but is compound in His oneness. Thus in Jesus' statement in John 10:30, He is not claiming that

He is the same person as the Father, but that He and the Father are one in their nature.

Implied Claims that He is God

--He claimed that to know Him was to know the Father:

*John 8:19 "Jesus answered, 'if you knew Me, you would know
    My Father also.'"*

--To see Him was to see God the Father:

*John 14:9 "Jesus said to him, 'Have I been so long with you,
    and yet you have not come to know Me, Philip? He who
    has seen Me has seen the Father.'"*

The Bible says that Jesus was the exact representation of God's nature. For years I thought of the Father as being one way and Jesus another. I thought of Jesus as "gentle Jesus, meek and mild" while the Father seemed more angry, a God of wrath. Maybe it's because when we're growing up we hear, "Just wait until your father gets home" when we misbehave that we associate the image of father with anger. But if Jesus is the exact representation of God's nature (as Hebrews 1:3 says), then whatever qualities we see in Jesus' life, the Father has the same, and in the same balance that we see in Jesus -- they aren't different. The same anger that we see at times in Jesus, is the anger of God; when He overturned the tables of the moneychangers, this reflects exactly how the Father felt. And when we see Jesus weeping over Jerusalem, the Father felt exactly the same way.

--To believe in Him, Jesus said, was to believe in God:

*John 12:44 "He who believes in Me does not believe in Me,
    but in Him who sent Me."*

--To receive Him was to receive God:

*Mark 9:37 "Whoever receives Me does not receive Me, but
    Him who sent Me."*

--To hate Him was to hate God:

John 15:23 "He who hates Me hates My Father also."

What Jesus Claimed by His Actions

In addition to the direct claims and the implied claims Jesus made, He claimed to be God indirectly by His actions, namely, Jesus did certain actions which are only appropriate for God to: He received worship, and He forgave sins.

When people worshiped Him, He received their worship. As background information, we should understand that the Jews were expressly forbidden to worship anyone but Jehovah. Exodus 34:14 says, "You shall not worship any other god." (This is also stated in the Ten Commandments and many other places). And notice Peter's reaction to being worshiped in Acts 10:25-26 "And when it came about that Peter entered, Cornelius met him, and fell at his feet and worshiped him. But Peter raised him up, saying, 'Stand up; I too am just a man.'" So this is a godly person's reaction to being worshiped. Also notice an angel's reaction to being worshiped in Revelation 19:10 "And I fell at his feet to worship him. And he said to me, 'Do not do that; I am a fellow servant of yours and your brethren who hold the testimony of Jesus; worship God.'"

Now let's look at Jesus' response when people worshiped Him.

Matthew 8:2 And behold, a leper came to Him, and bowed down to Him, saying, "Lord, if You are willing, You can make me clean."

John 9:38 And he [the man born blind] said, "Lord, I believe." And he worshiped Him.

John 20:27-28 Then He said to Thomas, "Reach here your finger, and see My hands; and reach here your hand, and put it into My side; and be not unbelieving, but

> *believing." Thomas answered and said to Him, "My Lord and my God!"*

Jesus received their worship, which only God should do!

Jesus also forgave people their sins.

> *Mark 2:5-7 And Jesus seeing their faith said to the paralytic, "My son, your sins are forgiven." But there were some of the scribes sitting there and reasoning in their hearts, "Why does this man speak that way? Who can forgive sins but God alone?"*

"We may begin with one of the central features of Jesus' itinerant ministry. He offered people 'forgiveness of sins,' not only by saying so but also in some of his most characteristic actions, namely, his welcome to and his feasting with 'sinners' of all sorts. He offered, in other words, the blessing that was normally obtained by going to the Temple. The immensity of this should not be missed… It was the offer of the new-covenant reality to which the Temple was the old-covenant signpost. That which you might obtain at the Temple—and would then need to obtain again after another round of sinning and impurity—you could have now and forever by accepting Jesus' welcome, by trusting in him, by following him. He was the personal embodiment of what the Temple stood for." (N.T. Wright, *The Challenge of Jesus*, IVP 1999, pp. 111-112.)

The Choice

"Depending on where you stand, that story is the tale of a prophet, a political agitator or the Messiah, the son of God made man. It is either a myth or the great news, either ancient history, fiction or Gospel. What's beyond dispute is that it has endured through the ages, while the pantheistic stories of other great civilizations became lost to all except those studying the classics." (Anna Quindlen, "Newsweek" Dec.26, 2005, p.128.)

"This is precisely what makes Jesus so unique. The whole range of both His life and His teaching can be subjected to the test of truth. ... The faith that the Bible speaks of is not antithetical to reason. ...Faith in the biblical sense is substantive, based on the knowledge that the One in whom that faith is placed has proven that He is worthy of that trust." (Ravi Zacharias, *Jesus Among Other Gods,* Word Publishing 2000, pp.55, 58.)

"...His eschatological preaching, his announcement that the kingdom was breaking in through his own work... Jesus in his entire public career was acting as if he were bringing about the new exodus. God's people were in slavery; he had heard their cry and was coming to rescue them. Just as the first exodus revealed the previously hidden meaning of YHWH's name, so now Jesus would reveal the person, one might say the personality, of YHWH in action, embodied in a human form." (N.T. Wright, *The Challenge of Jesus*, IVP 1999, pp.115-116.)

C.S. Lewis wrote: "I am trying here to prevent anyone saying the really foolish thing that people often say about Him: 'I'm ready to accept Jesus as a great moral teacher, but I don't accept His claim to be God.' That is the one thing we must not say. A man who was merely a man and said the sort of things Jesus said would not be a great moral teacher. He would either be a lunatic...or else he would be the devil of hell. You must make your choice. Either this man was, and is, the Son of God, or else a madman or something worse." (Quoted in *Evidence that Demands a Verdict*, CCC, 1972, p.107.)

Our Options

His claims were false and He knew ⟶ He is a liar.
His claims were false and He did not know ⟶ He is crazy.
His claims were true ⟶ He is God!

To reiterate, we are left with only three reasonable options as we think about this person Jesus. 1) If Jesus' claims were false and He knew it, we must conclude that He was a liar. 2) If His claims were false but He did not know it, we have to say He was mentally unbalanced -- a crazy person. 3) But if His claims were true, then our only option is that Jesus is God!

Now it's time to ask yourself this most important question: who do <u>you</u> say Jesus is?

Endnotes, chapter 1

A What is a word and the purpose of a word? It is a communication: a meaningful sound that takes a thought from one mind and makes the same thought occur in another mind. Therefore, Jesus' title the "Word of God" means that Jesus was God's ultimate communication to man. God couldn't do anything more to communicate with man than He did by becoming a man himself and living a life that demonstrated His nature to us.

B Reading "LORD" instead of "*Yahweh*" came from the Jewish custom of having such fear of breaking the command about taking the name of *Yahweh* in vain that they refused to say it out loud! Whenever a reader came to the word YHWH he would pronounce "Lord" ("*Adonai*") instead. That tradition carried over into our versions, and we English speakers are still reading "Lord" instead of the Hebrew "*Yahweh*" or "I am" in English. This has made it easy to forget that "LORD" is actually code-writing for "I am".

C A Hebrew speaker is confronted with the compound-oneness of God right from the first chapter of Genesis, because the Hebrew word we translate "God" is "*Elohim*," which is a plural noun. The "im" ending makes something plural in Hebrew, e.g. "cherubim" is plural for "cherub". But the surprising thing is that this plural noun *Elohim* is constantly used with verbs or adjectives in the singular. So starting in the first chapter of Genesis and reiterated thousands of times as the name *Elohim* is used, Hebrew emphasizes the compound nature of this Being who is one. A few examples in the English translations: Gen.3:22 "The man has become like one of Us, knowing good and evil," in Gen.11:7 "Let Us go down and there confuse their languages," and in Gen.1:26 "Then *Elohim* said, "Let us make man in our image."

Chapter Two
The Man Christ Jesus

To continue our investigation of who Jesus Christ was, read the following statement to see if you agree. "In eternity past Jesus was God, while on earth He put aside being God and became just a man, and after the resurrection He went back to being God." Do you agree or disagree? Stop and think about it for just a moment... I won't give away the answer quite yet.

In chapter one, we examined proof from the Bible that Jesus is God. In this chapter we'll look at what the Bible has to say about Jesus being a man.

Clear Scriptures that Jesus was a Man

In addition to being fully God, the New Testament also declares that He fully became a man, sharing our humanity with us.

John 1:14 And the Word became flesh and made His dwelling among us ...

Galatians 4:4 But when the fullness of the time came, God sent his Son, born of a woman...

Philippians 2:5-7 ...Christ Jesus, who, although He existed in the form of God, did not regard equality with God a thing to be grasped, but emptied Himself...being made in human likeness.

God became flesh -- He was born of a woman -- He emptied himself of "equality with God." That last statement is a difficult one, which we need to spend some time examining to be sure of what it is saying and what it is not saying.

In order to become a man, Philippians tells us that He emptied Himself -- but of what? What did He retain, and what did He lose as He put on human form? One thing that immediately comes to mind is that He had to empty Himself of His glory. During the Transfiguration (recorded in Matthew 17) three disciples saw Jesus in a glorified condition, and what they saw was very different from what they normally saw. It was so wonderful to be near this glory that Peter proposed camping out right there! You can sense that Peter was still enthralled by that experience when he refers to it years later in his second letter (see 2 Peter 1:16-18).

Jesus also emptied Himself of the power He had as the Son. By putting aside His own power, He became dependent on the power of the Holy Spirit and dependent on the Father's leading and speaking to Him. In other words, as a man He imposed certain limitations on Himself. He became dependent on the Holy Spirit to lead Him and empower Him in the same way that we are. How could He be our example and show us how to live if He had an independent power source that we can never have?

So He laid aside His glory as God, and His power as God.

This brings us to the crux of the matter: in addition to laying aside His power and glory, did He lay aside His <u>nature</u> as God, so that to become man He had to stop being God? Or was He God and man in one person during His life on earth?

Let's mull this over a bit. -- He is called "Emmanuel," that is, "God with us." -- He received worship, which only God should do. -- He used the name "I am." -- He said, "I and the Father are one," and didn't say, "I and the Father were one." -- When He spoke of praying to the Father, for instance in John 14:16, the word He used for "ask" means to ask from an equal to an equal, instead of another word available when asking something from a superior. [D]

Everything we learned in the first chapter proves that Jesus was God on earth among us. So we conclude that He did not stop being God in His nature, but He laid aside certain privileges as God and found Himself "in appearance as a man" (Philippians 2:8). As an illustration, when Peter the Great, Czar of Russia, was a young man he was extremely interested in learning about western Europe and especially about ships. So in 1697 Peter traveled under the pseudonym Peter Mikhailov, disguised himself and even apprenticed himself to a shipbuilder in Amsterdam. Did Peter stop being the Czar to do that? No, in who he was he was still Czar of Russia, but he had taken on the form of a servant. As a modern example, in the TV show "Undercover

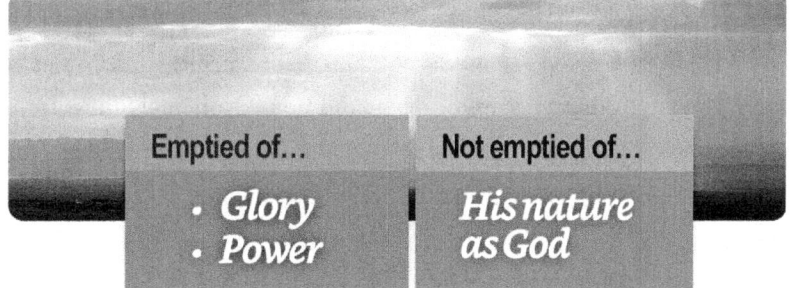

Boss" the CEOs of various companies put on disguises and work for a week as regular employees to discover what is going on inside their companies. They put on the "appearance" of a normal worker, but actually they are still the CEO!

After the Resurrection, Jesus got back all that He laid aside. His glory was restored:

John 17:5 And now, Father, glorify Me in your presence with the glory I had with You before the world began.

His power was restored:

Matthew 28:18 Then Jesus came to them and said, "All authority in heaven and on earth has been given to me."

So the glory and power He had laid aside He received again, along with His omniscience (Colossians 2:3), His omnipresence (Matthew 28:20; Matthew 18:20), etc. Everything He had laid aside was restored to Him.

This transition leads us to the next question. After His resurrection, did He lay aside being man, and go back to being God just as before? Let's think about this in light of

> 1 Timothy 2:5 *For there is one God, and one mediator also between God and men, the <u>man</u> Christ Jesus.*

Before you read on, think about when this scripture was written. Was it written while Jesus was still in his ministry on earth, or years after the resurrection?

In eternity past, Jesus was not a man. In eternity future, does He stop being man, or by becoming a man did He take on humanness for all eternity, so that He continues to be God and man combined? Let's vote on it: do you think He became God only, or God/man? Hopefully you voted for the second, because Paul's letter to Timothy is written after the resurrection, and calls Him "the man Christ Jesus" in the present tense. So at that time, after the resurrection and ascension, Jesus is called a man. Another proof: Stephen at his martyrdom (Acts 7:56) looks into heaven and calls Jesus "the Son of Man." Then we also have

> Hebrews 2:11 *For both He who sanctifies and those who are sanctified are all from one [one nature]; for which reason He is not ashamed to call them brethren.*

The entire section of Hebrews 2:10-18 is meant to show us that Jesus had to made like us to be our High Priest—which He continues to be for us right now. And the glorified human body of Jesus continues into eternity: He told Thomas to touch Him and be convinced after the Resurrection (John 20:27). If you can bear with me for one last proof, 1 Corinthians 15:45 and 15:47 calls Jesus "the last Adam" and "the second man": signifying that through His work the curse of human nature (the Adamic nature, "the last Adam") would be done away with, and a new

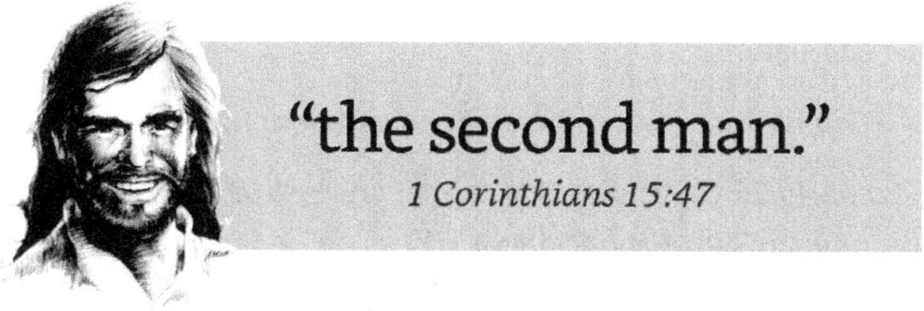

"the second man."
1 Corinthians 15:47

type of man ("the second man") would emerge. Jesus is (present tense) the second man.

> "**Definition of Chalcedon**" (451 AD) "Following, then, the holy fathers, we unite in teaching all men to confess the one and only Son, our Lord Jesus Christ. This selfsame one is perfect both in deity and in humanness; this selfsame one is also actually God and actually man, with a rational soul and a body. He is of the same reality as God as far as his deity is concerned and of the same reality as we ourselves as far as his humanness is concerned; thus like us in all respects, sin only excepted. Before time began he was begotten of the Father, in respect of his deity, and now in these 'last days,' for us and on behalf of our salvation, this selfsame one was born of Mary the virgin, who is God-bearer in respect of his humanness. ..."

Let's take a brief detour and ask, what will we be in eternity? Will we be "like Jesus" and therefore somehow become God and man in one? No! Never! We will be glorified men, but we will never be God. Walter Martin, the famous researcher of cults and author of The Kingdom of the Cults, said that every person needs to know two things: 1) God is God, and 2) you never will be! That sums it up nicely and is so important to know! Some people misinterpret 1 John 3:2 "We know that, when He appears, we shall be like Him" to say that we will become gods. But in the context of the rest of Scripture, what this must mean is that we will become like Him in our character, but not become like Him in His God-nature.

God has no equal, as the next verses make clear.

Isaiah 40:25 "To whom will you compare me? Or who is my equal?" says the Holy One. (NIV)

Isaiah 43:10-12 "You are my witnesses," declares the Lord, "and my servant whom I have chosen, so that you may know and believe me and understand that I am he. Before me no god was formed, nor will there be one after me. I, even I, am the Lord, and apart from me there is no savior. ... You are my witnesses," declares the Lord, "that I am God." (NIV)

Colossians 1:18b ...that in everything He might have the supremacy. (NIV)

Through Jesus we can become partakers of God's Spirit (Acts 2:38-39) and even His nature (2 Peter 1:4), but His <u>position</u> as God is His alone.

How else can we prove to ourselves that Jesus was fully a man?

Jesus Experienced Common Human Experiences

-- Humans grow up, and Jesus grew up.

Luke 2:51 And He went down with them, and came to Nazareth; and He continued in subjection to them; and His mother treasured all these things in her heart.

-- Humans experience physical weakness, and Jesus experienced physical weakness.

John 4:6 Jesus therefore, being wearied from His journey, was sitting thus by the well.

> *Mark 4:37-38 And there arose a fierce gale of wind, and the waves were breaking over the boat so much that the boat was already filling up. And He Himself was in the stern, asleep on the cushion.*

As we can see, He submitted to His parents -- He became tired and thirsty -- He was so tired He slept through a storm! [E]

Very early in Church history an error called Gnosticism arose, which claimed that Jesus looked like a man but wasn't really a man, that He was a spirit without real human form -- if he walked on the sand he left no footprints, for instance. In the Apostle John's first letter, John is answering this error when he emphasizes that he writes about what they themselves had seen and what their hands handled concerning the Word (1 John 1:1). John wanted to make it clear that Jesus was solid and touchable to counteract the error of the Gnostics.

Jesus had laid aside the glory and power that He had as God and became weak and dependent as a man, just as we are. He had to share our humanity so that He could become our mediator with God.

> *Hebrews 2:14 & 17 Since the children have flesh and blood, He too shared in their humanity ... he had to be made like His brothers in every way, in order that He might become a merciful and faithful high priest in service to God, and that He might make atonement for the sins of the people. (NIV)*

> *Hebrews 5:8-9 Although He was a son, He learned obedience from what He suffered and, once made perfect, He became the source for eternal salvation to all who obey Him... (NIV)*

Wait a minute!! The passage reads, "once made perfect," but I thought Jesus was always perfect!? Is it implying there was some imperfection, some sin in Jesus? The Greek word clears up any misunderstanding. The word here for "made perfect" means "adapted or fitted for a task." So Jesus was always sinless, but He had to be fitted for the task of salvation through obedience to the Father's will and through suffering.

Someone asked what part of His human-ness Jesus took with Him to heaven. That's a difficult question, but I would say that in addition to His body He certainly took His experiences (symbolized, maybe, by the wounds He still had after the resurrection?); it is these experiences that equipped Him for His present role as our High Priest.

-- Humans have emotions, and Jesus had emotions.

Popular movies may portray Him as perpetually calm, with a measured lack of emotion, but the Gospels paint a different picture, of a charismatic and winsome personality. He rejoiced greatly at the disciples' success (Luke 10:21) and could keep a crowd spellbound for three days, even after they ran out of food (Mark 8:2). His speaking ability was so compelling that soldiers sent to arrest him refused to do it: "Never did a man speak the way this man speaks," was the answer they gave their superiors (John 7:46). He got angry at people's hardness of heart toward those who were suffering (Mark 3:5), and delivered scathing rebukes to the religiously smug (Luke 11:42-44). He wept openly, in public (Luke 19:41; John 11:35). At Gethsemane He was overcome by sorrow (Mark 14:34). People as diverse as children and tax collectors liked to be with Jesus, which would hardly be the case if He had been icily emotionless.

Jesus Was Tempted

Humans are tempted and Jesus was no exception.

Matthew 4:1-11 records one time Jesus was tempted:

> *(verses 1-3) Then Jesus was led up by the Spirit into the wilderness to be tempted by the devil. And after He had fasted forty days and forty nights, He then became hungry. And the tempter came and said to Him, "If You*

are the Son of God, command that these stones become bread."

[He's being tempted to use His own power as the Son of God, not the Holy Spirit's power.]

(verses 4-6) But He answered and said, "It is written, 'MAN SHALL NOT LIVE ON BREAD ALONE, BUT ON EVERY WORD THAT PROCEEDS OUT OF THE MOUTH OF GOD.'" Then the devil took Him into the holy city; and he had Him stand on the pinnacle of the temple, and said to Him, "If You are the Son of God throw Yourself down; for it is written, 'HE WILL GIVE HIS ANGELS CHARGE CONCERNING YOU'; and 'ON THEIR HANDS THEY WILL BEAR YOU UP, LEST YOU STRIKE YOUR FOOT AGAINST A STONE.'"

[Who is quoting scripture here? The devil is, and quoting it accurately. The devil will quote scripture in the voice inside your mind to you also, but always in a wrong application. We have to know which scripture to apply in the circumstances, as Jesus did.]

(verses 7-11) Jesus said to him, "On the other hand, it is written, 'YOU SHALL NOT PUT THE LORD YOUR GOD TO THE TEST.'" Again, the devil took Him to a very high mountain, and showed Him all the kingdoms of the world, and their glory; and he said to Him, "All these things will I give You, if You fall down and worship me." Then Jesus said to him, "Be gone, Satan! For it is written, 'YOU SHALL WORSHIP THE LORD YOUR GOD, AND SERVE HIM ONLY.'" Then the devil left Him; and behold, angels came and began to minister to Him.

Deuteronomy 6:13	Deuteronomy 6:16	Deuteronomy 8:3
Worship God only.	*Not force a test on the Lord.*	*Not live on bread alone.*

Did you notice the one phrase Jesus used each time He was tempted? He said, "It is written." The scriptures Jesus quoted to combat the enemy's thoughts are from Deuteronomy, not your best-known scriptures in the world! Jesus really knew His Bible! This may be a tip for us to have success in resisting temptation.

But there is one vast difference between Jesus being tempted and everyone else. Hebrews 4:15 says that He was "tempted in every way, just as we are -- yet was without sin." Jesus was tempted in every way, but never yielded to the temptations -- He never sinned!

Jesus, the Perfect Man

Look at the description of Jesus' character in

Hebrews 7:26 For it was fitting that we should have such a
high priest, holy, innocent, undefiled, separated from
sinners and exalted to the heavens.

Imagine! Never a wrong thought or motive. Never a word spoken out of turn or one that He was sorry about later. Never selfish, never proud. He lived such an upright life that He challenged His detractors with (John 8:46) "Can any of you prove me guilty of sin?"

In eternity past Jesus was...	During 33 years Jesus was...	At present Jesus is...
God	*God*	*God*
God + man	*God + man*	*God + man*
man	*man*	*man*

Jesus, God and Man in One

From what we've studied in chapters one and two, we can now conclude that: in eternity past Jesus was God; He came to earth to become God and man combined in one person; and now He continues as God and man in one.

Endnotes, chapter 2

D In John 11:22 Martha says, *"Even now I know that whatever You ask of God, God will give You,"* using the Greek word *aitein*, from *aiteo*, which means to ask by an inferior from a superior: a child asking a parent (Mt.7:9), a beggar asking a potential donor (Acts 3:2), a man asking God (Mt.7:7; John 14:13, 14; James 1:5). But Jesus never used this word when He spoke of His asking or praying. When He said in *John 14:16, "I will ask the Father"* He used *erotao*, to ask from equal to equal, which He also used in John 17:9, 15, & 20. By using *aitein*, Martha showed that she did not yet understand who Jesus was.

E How Jesus could sleep with water washing over the boat? Wouldn't the water splash on Him and wake Him up? Archaeology solved this puzzle just a few years ago. In a severe drought, the Sea of Galilee receded and two brothers discovered the prow of an old boat sticking up through the mud. They alerted archaeologists, who excavated and found it was a first-century fishing boat which was 27 feet long by 7 feet wide at the beam. The rear of the boat was covered over by a platform on which the steersman would stand, and under the stern the ballast bag was kept ("the cushion" referred to in Mark 4). So Jesus slept under the covered platform, protected from the waves. Once again science continues to confirm the historical accuracy of the New Testament.

Chapter Three
Why Jesus Came

In the first two chapters we saw that Jesus Christ is fully God and fully man. Now we want to examine why Jesus came to earth.

Mankind's Condition

What is the nature of man? Do you believe that man, deep down, is basically good or basically evil?

> *Romans 3:9-18 What then? Are we better than they? Not at all; for we have already charged that both Jews and Greeks are all under sin; as it is written, "There is none righteous, not even one; there is none who understands, there is none who seeks for God; all have turned aside, together they have become useless; there is none who does good, there is not even one." "Their throat is an open grave, with their tongues they keep deceiving," "The poison of asps is under their lips;" "Whose mouth is full of cursing and bitterness;" "Their feet are swift to shed blood, destruction and misery are in their paths, and the path of peace have they not known." "There is no fear of God before their eyes."*

This passage describes man's mouth as "full of cursing and bitterness." So many people have a foul mouth! When I was twelve years old, my dad committed his life to Christ, and in one day he stopped cursing. I'll tell you, I noticed the difference! We all know what a mouth "full of cursing" sounds like, but what does a mouth full of "bitterness" sound like? That mouth would be negative, complaining, whining, "poor me," or vindictive and expressing a desire for revenge.

Man's feet are characterized in the passage above as "swift to shed blood." Very quickly murder came into the narrative of the book of Genesis. How quickly? By the second generation! A few generations after that, a man named Lamech boasts, "I have killed a man for wounding me, and a boy for injuring me" (Genesis 4:23). Later the commandment, "eye for eye, tooth for tooth" (Exodus 21:24) placed limits on how much retribution could be demanded, restricting our vengeful impulses. This was necessary because mankind's normal nature, illustrated by Lamech, is that if someone insults us we want to take the ultimate revenge -- to kill them! If someone cuts you off in traffic, you want to ram their car! Haven't you felt this? This is our human nature.

Before man's eyes there is no fear of God (v.18). How do you tell that there is no fear of God? If the fear of God is to hate evil (Proverbs 8:13), and we see no hatred of evil, then we conclude that there is no fear of God in front of people's "eyes," i.e. their planning, dreaming, wanting, and desiring.

Then look at the general words that describe mankind's condition: misery -- no peace -- useless to God -- turned aside -- none that does good. We humans are in a sad state!

> *Ephesians 2:1-3 And you were dead in your trespasses and sins, in which you formerly walked according to the course of this world* [trespasses and sins are the normal "course of this world"], *according to the prince of the power of the air, of the spirit that is now working in the sons of disobedience.* [What spirit is that? Satan. What is Satan's realm? Is it hell? Hell is a place of punishment prepared for him and his colleagues. His realm is "roaming around on the earth" as it says in Job 1:7.] *Among them we too all formerly lived in the lusts of our flesh, indulging the desires of the flesh and of*

> *the mind, and were by nature children of wrath, even as the rest.*
>
> *Titus 3:3 For we also once were foolish ourselves, disobedient, deceived, enslaved to various lusts and pleasures, spending our life in malice and envy, hateful, hating one another.*

Romans 3:23 sums up the condition of mankind by saying "for all have sinned and fall short of the glory of God."

Do you agree? What does it mean to "fall short of the glory of God"? The most basic definition of sin is "to miss the mark", like an arrow that falls short before it reaches its target. We think of sin as disobedience; God thinks of what might have been. God thinks of the wonderful glory man would have had and the fellowship man would have enjoyed with Him and with each other. At a mental hospital I visited a young man who destroyed his mind by sniffing paint thinner. This 18-year-old was unpredictably violent, his thinking was confused and his memory muddled, and he felt bad all the time. MRI tests revealed that his mind was so damaged that he has no possibility of a normal life and will have to live out his days in an institution. When I think of him, instead of thinking, "What a sinner!" I think, "What a waste!" It's a vivid illustration to me that sin is "missing the mark."

The Old Testament uses two other words along with "sin" that round out our understanding of human nature: "transgression" and "iniquity" (see Psalm 51:1-2 and other passages). "Transgression" is the Hebrew word for rebellion and "iniquity" means depravity or twisted-ness. So sin is rebellion against God, it is being twisted or deformed in our character, and it is missing the mark of what God had for us.

How did mankind get this way? In a word, we were <u>born</u> wrong. We inherited this nature with its inclination to sin from our ancestors.

How many of us as parents have been astonished by the lies our children invent? It's especially startling the first time it happens. I remember it with ours. At age two it's pretty obvious when they are lying -- there's the chocolate all around the child's mouth and the missing candy bar. Parent: "Did you do this?" Child: "No." The child lies! It's astonishing how easily it comes to them! You don't have to teach children to lie; something inside them teaches them to lie and cover up. I remember when one of our daughters had her first tantrum. We said "No" about something (I don't remember what), and she threw herself down, crying, pounding her fists and kicking those little white Stride-Rite shoes into the kitchen floor. It was a classic tantrum! I stood there observing this and thought, "This is amazing, where did she learn that?" She hadn't seen me or her mom model this behavior for her, yet she was able to invent it herself!

We are born wrong: when Adam and Eve sinned, they completed human nature with this bend toward evil and passed it down to their offspring.

> *By the transgression of the one, death reigned through the one... through one transgression there resulted condemnation to all men (Romans 5:17, 18).*

So, after reviewing what the Bible says about man, would you conclude that mankind is basically good or basically evil? It sounds harsh, but I have to conclude we are basically evil. Jesus confirmed it when He said, "If you, being evil, can give good gifts to your children..." (Luke 11:13). He also said, "No one is good except God alone" (Luke 18:19).

At this point in history it's not hard to convince people of the evil that lies within the humanity. A hundred years ago it wasn't as easy. In the late 1800s and early 1900s a strong teaching came along that blamed all the evils of mankind on the environment. It said that if we just clean up the slums, change the ghettos, build playgrounds for the children, etc., that the inherent good in man would come out; just educate and bring culture to people, and all the social ills will be resolved. At that point in history it looked like man was headed up. But then came the World Wars, Nazism and Communism, 'ethnic cleansing' and terrorism. The capacity we humans have to be cruel is truly frightening, and acting in a civilized way may be merely a thin veneer.

The result of all this is that "Your iniquities have separated you from your God" (Isaiah 59:2). The result of sin is a separation from God.

Romans 6:23 For the wages of sin is death.

J.B. Phillips' translation puts it, "Sin pays its servants: the wage is death." Sin pays, and the paycheck is death! We think of death as ceasing, because that is what we see happen to the body, but a better definition would be that death is separation: physical death is separation of the body from the soul; eternal death is separation of the person from God. The soul lives on forever (Matthew 25:46 "these will go away into eternal punishment"). The only options are eternal life with God or eternal death, i.e. eternal separation from God and everything good.

God's Dilemma -- Love or Justice?

This left God with a dilemma: His love made Him want to do one thing, but His justice demanded something else. Because of His love He wanted to overlook His creatures' transgressions, but His justice required that the penalty for sin, death to all sinners, be carried out! "How can I give you up! How can I surrender you and cast you off!...My heart recoils within Me, My compassions are kindled together." (Hosea 11:8, *Amplified Bible*)

God's Solution

God's solution is so extraordinary that it's called the gospel, the "good news". In our wildest imaginings we would not have come up with the idea God had: God Himself would become a man, live a sinless life, then give up that life as a payment for sin! He Himself would pay the penalty for sin!

> *Isaiah 53:6 and the Lord has laid on him the iniquity of us all.*

> *John 3:16-18a For God so loved the world, that He gave His only begotten Son, that whoever believes in Him should not perish, but have eternal life. For God did not send the Son into the world to judge the world, but that the world should be saved through Him. He who believes in Him is not judged.*

The Son came not as a judge, but as a Savior. Because of His coming, those who believe can be rescued from perishing.

> *John 12:23-24, 27-33 And Jesus answered them, saying, "The hour has come for the Son of Man to be glorified. Truly, truly, I say to you, unless a grain of wheat falls into the earth and dies, it remains by itself alone; but if it dies, it bears much fruit. ...(verse 27) Now My soul has become troubled; and what shall I say, 'Father, save Me from this hour'? But for this purpose I came to this hour. Father, glorify Thy name." There came therefore a voice out of heaven: "I have both glorified it, and will glorify it again." The multitude therefore, who stood by and heard it, were saying that it had thundered; others were saying, "An angel has spoken to Him." Jesus answered and said, "This voice has not come for My sake, but for your sakes. Now judgment is upon this world; now the ruler of this world shall be cast out. And I, if I be lifted up from the earth, will draw all men to Myself." But He*

> *was saying this to indicate the kind of death by which He was to die.*

Notice the connection between verse 32 "lifted up from the earth" and verse 33 "He was saying this to indicate the kind of death by which He was to die." What's the connection? Jesus predicts that He would die by being "lifted up," that is the He would die on a cross, lifted up from the earth. Isn't this a given? Not at all! The normal Jewish method of execution was stoning. (A few years later Stephen, the first Christian martyr, died in Jerusalem by stoning.) Only because the Roman authorities were in Jerusalem to maintain control during the holiday when Jesus was arrested did He die by the Roman method of execution.

In verse 27 Jesus says, "for this purpose I came." What purpose is that? The purpose of dying!

> *I Timothy 1:15 "It is a trustworthy statement, deserving full acceptance, that Christ Jesus came into the world to save sinners."*

Why did Jesus come? To save sinners by dying on the cross for their sins.

Our Response

How can we respond to this tremendous thing God has done in becoming a man, living a perfect life, and then taking the punishment for sin that we deserve, so that we can be forgiven? I think we can sum up in three words what we need to do: repent – believe – receive.

Repent means "think again" and "turn around." If your life is headed in a wrong direction, it doesn't have to continue going that way! You can rethink it and change direction. There is a way out!

> *Matthew 4:17 From that time Jesus began to preach and say, "Repent, for the kingdom of heaven is at hand."*

Acts 3:19 Repent therefore and return, that your sins may be wiped away.

If we will repent, i.e. change our thinking and direction, we can be forgiven. But if we deny that we have sinned, the next scripture tells us that we are calling God a liar!

1 John 1:8-10 If we say that we have no sin, we are deceiving ourselves, and the truth is not in us. If we confess our sins, He is faithful and righteous to forgive us our sins and to cleanse us from all unrighteousness. If we say that we have not sinned, we make Him a liar, and His word is not in us.

If we confess our sins, God promises to forgive us and cleanse us.

Next, we **believe**.

Romans 10:9 If you confess with your mouth Jesus as Lord, and believe in your heart that God raised Him from the dead, you shall be saved.

It's a promise from God! We confess Jesus as our Lord and believe that God raised Him from the dead - which means He is alive, right now!

And we **receive** Jesus into our lives.

John 1:12 To as many as received Him, He gave the right to become children of God.

If you receive Jesus as your Savior and Lord, you are now a born-again child of God, and God is truly your Father. The decision to receive Jesus as your Lord and Savior is the most important decision you can make here on earth. If you've never done it, you can do it right now.

Chapter Four
Justified by Faith

What "Justified" Means

"Justified" is one of those Bible terms that we don't use every day. It is primarily a legal term. To justify someone means to declare that they are innocent or to make them righteous. If such a word existed in English, it would be "righteousify" - to make righteous. Even in Old Testament times they knew of this possibility, as the psalmist said, "Blessed is the man whose sin the Lord does not count against him" (Ps.32:2, NIV). That's it, exactly! Happy is the person whose sins God does not write on the account; blessed is the person that God declares innocent!

> "The most fundamental matter for us to grasp about justification by faith is that it refers to the way God sees us, not the way we see ourselves. ...Justification is forensic, that is, it is entirely a legal matter. ...What is legal may not sound very relevant. But once you realize we are talking about the way God will judge you – that matters." (R.T. Kendall, *Once Saved, Always Saved*, Authentic Media, 2005, p.44.)

Who Can Be Justified?

Romans 4:5 contains an astonishing title for God. It describes God as one "who justifies the ungodly." We would expect it to say that God "justifies the innocent," but instead we read that God justifies ungodly people! Listen to the comments of a famous preacher of the late 1800s:

> "When a lawyer comes into court, if he is an honest man, he desires to plead the case of an innocent person

and justify him before the court from the things which are falsely laid to his charge. It should be the lawyer's object to justify the innocent person, and he should not attempt to screen the guilty party. It is not man's right nor in his power to truly justify the guilty. This is a miracle reserved for the Lord alone. God, the infinitely just Sovereign, knows that there is not a man upon earth who does good and does not sin. Therefore, in the splendor of His love, He undertakes the task, not of justifying the just as of justifying the ungodly. God has devised ways and means of making the ungodly man to stand justly accepted before Him. He has set up a system by which with perfect justice He can treat the guilty as if he had been free from offense; yes, can treat him as if he were wholly free from sin." (Charles H. Spurgeon, *All of Grace*, Moody Press, pp. 9-11.)

What are these "ways and means" Spurgeon refers to, by which an ungodly person can stand before God as if he had never sinned?

The Wrong Approach to be Declared Innocent

Let's first see if we can eliminate one path that leads in the wrong direction, the path of trying to be righteous by our own good deeds.

> *Titus 3:5 He saved us, not on the basis of deeds which we have done in righteousness, but according to His mercy.*
>
> *Romans 3:20 By the works of law no mortal man will be declared innocent.*
>
> *Gal.2:16 Knowing that a man is not justified by the works of the Law ...since by the works of the Law shall no mortal man be justified.*
>
> *Gal.2:21 I do not nullify the grace of God; for if righteousness comes through the Law, then Christ died needlessly.*

You mean you don't earn your way into heaven?! That's right! Paul is very bold to say that if righteousness could be gained by keeping the law, then Christ did not need to die! If there were another way for people to become righteous (even one other way), then Christ would not have died!

Imagine for a moment that we are all competing in a vertical-leap contest. Some of us can jump ten inches in the air, some twenty-two inches or more. Everyone is impressed by the athletes who can jump higher than the rest. We then discover that the goal of the contest isn't to compete against each other but to leap to a helicopter hovering hundreds of feet above! The difference of a few inches becomes totally meaningless! Some thought they were doing well, but that was only because they were comparing themselves with other people. When we see that God's standard is a sin-free life, then we realize that our works fall hopelessly short of getting us to heaven.

The Purpose of the Law of Moses

Most Christians have a lot of confusion about their relationship to the Old Testament Law. How does the Apostle Paul explain the purpose of that Law?

> *Romans 3:19-20 Now we know that whatever the Law says, it speaks to those who are under the Law, that every mouth may be closed, and all the world may become accountable to God; because by the works of the Law no flesh will be justified in His sight; for through the Law comes the knowledge of sin.*

> *Romans 7:7 Indeed I would not have known what sin was except through the law.*

The Law came to make us aware of our sinfulness, to silence every objection and show people we are accountable to God. But no person --not one-- will be justified through the works the Law prescribes. God gave the Law not to make us righteous but to make us aware of our unrighteousness.

> *Galatians 3:23-25 But before faith came, we were kept in custody under the law, being shut up to the faith which was later to be revealed. Therefore the Law has become our tutor [literally "child-conductor"] to lead us to Christ, that we may be justified by faith. But now that faith has come, we are no longer under a tutor.*

The law is a temporary measure with the express purpose of leading us to Christ so that we can be justified by faith. These verses compare the law to a tutor who prepares a child for adulthood. (Even in Old Testament times the law had a system of sacrifices for forgiveness, which constantly emphasized to people their need for a sacrifice to take their place because of their disobedience. All these sacrifices pointed ultimately to the one perfect sacrifice: Christ.) And did you catch the last part of verse 25? We are no longer under the law!

> The more we try to keep the Law the more our weakness is manifest ... until it is clearly demonstrated to us that we are hopelessly weak. God knew it all along, but we did not, and so God had to bring us through painful experiences to a recognition of the fact. We need to have our weakness proved to ourselves beyond dispute. That is why God gave us the Law.
>
> No, the Law was not given in the expectation that we would keep it. It was given in the full knowledge that we would break it, and when we have broken it so completely as to be convinced or our utter need, then the Law has served its purpose. It has been our schoolmaster to bring us to Christ. (Watchman Nee, *The Normal Christian Life*, CLC 1966, pp.110-111.)

Was the Law given to justify us? No, it was given to condemn us! The Law came to show us our need, so we would be ready to accept God's answer--His Son--when He came!

The Right Approach to be Declared Innocent

Acts 13:38-39 Therefore let it be known to you, brethren, that through Him forgiveness of sins is proclaimed to you, and through Him everyone who believes is freed [literally, "justified"] from all things from which you could not be freed through the Law of Moses.

The marvelous news is that justification comes totally apart from good works. Consider the next verse's description of <u>how</u> justification happens:

Romans 3:24 being justified as a gift by His grace through the redemption that is in Christ Jesus.

Being declared innocent or made righteous comes to a person <u>as a gift</u>! If someone gives you a gift, how much does it cost you? Nothing! That's worth repeating: gifts do not cost anything, and justification is a gift. The verse goes on to say that justification is "by <u>grace</u> through <u>redemption</u>." A couple definitions of these Bible words will help us here. "Grace" means "unmerited favor," i.e. favor from God we don't deserve. We are justified as we receive favor from God that we don't deserve. Our next word, "redemption", means "to buy back a captive for a demanded price." Imagine that you were kidnapped and a ransom note was sent to your relatives. The note would say that the kidnappers were holding you as their prisoner, and certain demands must be met for you to be released, usually a specific sum of money. The price for your freedom is the redemption money, and at the time of your release, you become redeemed. That is exactly what Jesus did by justifying us: we were held captive by sin to do evil, a ransom was paid which we didn't deserve (the "grace" part), and we were bought back from being prisoners of sin.

Romans 3:28 A man is justified by faith apart from works.

Again, justification doesn't happen by works but does happen by faith: instead of working for salvation, we trust God to do it for us. Hopefully these passages are making it crystal clear to us that we can't work for salvation (justification), but that we can trust God to give justification to us as a gift!

> *Romans 5:9 Having now been justified by His blood.*

What does being declared innocent "by blood" mean? Leviticus 17:11 says, "For the life of the flesh is in the blood," therefore "blood" represents a life, and in Exodus 12:13 God says, "When I see the blood I will pass over you." Exodus 12 is the record of the first Passover. At the first Passover, each family selected a lamb, then killed it and sprinkled the blood outside their door. Inside the house they roasted and ate the sacrifice while being fully dressed, ready to leave Egypt. During the night an angel traveled through Egypt, examining each house. If any household did not have the blood outside their door, the angel entered and killed the first-born. But God said, "When I see the blood, I will pass over," meaning that because of the sacrifice of a lamb and the blood He sees, God's judgment would pass by and not come to that household. The blood of the lamb was outside the door for God to see; the people inside didn't see the blood as they ate the sacrifice, but God's angel did. Because of the blood of the sacrifice (because the life of the sacrifice had been offered for those inside), judgment did not come there. The New Testament tells us that the lamb represents Christ and the blood pictures His giving up His life by taking the punishment for sin that we deserved.

> *1 Peter 1:18-19 You were not redeemed with perishable things like silver or gold from your futile way of life inherited from your forefathers, but with precious blood, as of a lamb unblemished and spotless, of Christ.*

> *Hebrews 9:12 And not through the blood of goats and calves, but through His own blood, He entered the holy place once for all, having obtained eternal redemption.*

If we watch a person praying the prayer of salvation, all we see and hear is a person repenting for their sins and asking Jesus to be the Master of their life. But if we could put on some type of miraculous eyeglasses that allowed us to see into the spiritual realm (the reality that co-exists with our world, but of which we are usually unaware), we would watch the Holy Spirit come to this praying person with a basin containing the blood of Jesus, and sprinkle Jesus' blood on his innermost spiritual being! The blood is on the person's heart for God to see. And when God sees the blood of Jesus, His judgment passes by! That's what the Bible means when it says we were "justified by His blood."

Ephesians 2:8-9 For by grace you have been saved through faith; and that not of yourselves, it is the gift of God; not as a result of works, that no one should boast.

Again: by grace (undeserved favor) through faith (we trust God for it) as a gift (free) and not as a result of works (we can't earn it).

Maybe you've noticed that we are mixing two causes of our justification, the objective cause and the instrumental cause, or the "by" cause and the "through" cause. We are saved by grace, by the blood, through faith. Objectively, our salvation rests on what Jesus accomplished plus nothing. Instrumentally, our salvation rests on our faith plus nothing. Both must be present or the person is not saved: if Jesus died for their punishment but they do not put their trust in Him, they are not saved; and if they place their faith in the wrong thing, for instance their own works as their hope of salvation, they also are not saved. We must have faith as the channel to receive the gift God offers, and the faith must be depending on Jesus to save us. Jesus' life and death were sufficient for God to declare innocent everyone who trusts in that life and death for their salvation. Nothing else is needed. In fact, to think that we need to add to Jesus' work with our own works, devalues what Jesus accomplished. In Jesus' day they had a word, "teleo," that was written across debts that were paid: it was this very word that Jesus cried from the cross, "Finished!" And it is!

Let's summarize what we've learned about justification. God declares people innocent because of favor they doesn't deserve, as they realize that they can never earn salvation, but trust God to freely give it to them because Jesus took their punishment.

Chapter Five
The Three Parts of Salvation

The Three-in-oneness of God and of Man

In the first chapter we discussed Jesus' statement that He and the Father are one, and understood that He spoke about a compound oneness. Another way of expressing this is that God is called "the Trinity," the Trinity or Three-in-One, consisting of the Father, the Son, and the Holy Spirit. How can we begin to comprehend the three-in-oneness of God? (If God were our creation instead of the other way around, we would come up with something simpler! But it makes sense that it can be difficult for a created being to understand its Creator.)

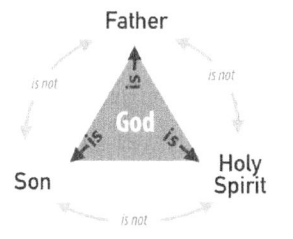

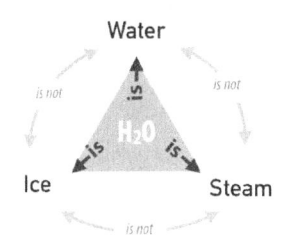

A picture that helps me is H_2O, which can be ice, water, or steam. Ice is not water, water isn't steam, and steam isn't ice, but all are H_2O; all share the same nature. In the same way the Son is not the Father and the Father is not the Holy Spirit, etc., but all are God. (One weakness of this analogy is that water, ice, and steam change from one form to another, which is not true of the persons of the Trinity. A strength of the analogy is that all three have the identical nature, H_2O.)

Do we ever find all three persons of the Trinity present in one Bible passage? Yes! At the baptism of Jesus we see Jesus being baptized, the Holy Spirit coming down in the form of a dove, and the Father speaking out of heaven: Matthew 3:16-17 "And after being baptized, Jesus went up immediately from the water; and behold, the heavens were opened, and he saw the Spirit of God descending as a dove, and coming upon Him, and behold, a voice out of the heavens, saying, 'This is My beloved Son, in whom I am well-pleased.'" In another passage, in chapters four and five of Revelation we again see all three: God the Father sitting on the throne, the seven Spirits (the Holy Spirit) like flames before the throne, and the Lamb (Jesus) next to the throne. (These are not the only times we find all three present.)

Something else may help us understand how three can be one, because not only is God a three-in-one, but man is also. Genesis 1:26 "Then God said, 'Let us make man in our image.'" Making man in God's image meant, among other things, that the three-in-one God made a three-in-one man. We inherently understand that we are more than just a body; we have a sense that we have a soul in addition to a body. So we think of ourselves as a more than just a body. Sometimes we think of the inside part as heart and mind.   Heart, mind, and body would correspond to the Bible's description of man as having spirit (heart), soul (mind), and body: 1 Thessalonians 5:23 "may your spirit and soul and body be preserved complete." So man has a spirit, a soul, and a body combined into one person.

Often people use "spirit" and "soul" inter-changeably, as if they are merely synonyms for the same thing. But evidently they are not the same, because Hebrews 4:12 describes the word of God "sharper than any two-edged sword, and piercing as far as the division of soul and spirit." If God's Word can be used to point out the division between them, then they are not the same. There is a division between them! And yet, that division may not be easy to determine: the fact that they are used as an example of how "sharp" the Word of God is, means that we will have to be precise in our use of the Bible to divide the two. In other words, the Word of God is SO sharp that it can even be used to point out the distinction between soul and spirit.

What is the difference, then, between soul and spirit? The best quick definition I have heard is that my body allows me to be conscious of the physical world, i.e. the senses of my physical makeup allow me to interact and be aware of the physical world. My soul is the part of me that allows me to become self-aware, i.e. through which I am conscious of self: my mind, will, and emotions. My spirit (once reborn and therefore activated) is the part of me that allows me to interact and be conscious of God and the spiritual world.

In the description of the creation of man we recognize the three parts of mankind being created:

Genesis 2:7 Then the LORD *God formed man of dust from the ground* [body], *and breathed into his nostrils the breath of life* [spirit; the Hebrew word '*nephesh*' means both 'breath' and 'spirit'], *and man became a living soul.*

Differentiating between the three parts of man is critically important to understanding salvation.

Three Parts of Salvation

Thus far we have focused on our initial salvation and how it happens, and now we're ready to investigate other aspects of salvation. For although we normally think of "salvation" and "justification" as synonymous, they are not; salvation includes much more than justification only. "Salvation" is a broad term that includes three parts: justification, sanctification, and glorification. Briefly stated,

--justification is a legal transaction in which a person is declared innocent;

--sanctification is the transformation of our actions and character to come into conformity with God's will and character; and

--glorification will be the changing of our bodies into eternal bodies.

Justification brings freedom from the penalty of sin; sanctification brings freedom from the power sin has over us now; and glorification will one day bring freedom from the presence of sin.

Justification is our initial experience of salvation. In the last chapter we studied justification in detail and saw that it is a one-time, instantaneous event. When a person turns to the Lord and receives forgiveness, that individual is released from the penalty of sin and is "born again" as the Spirit gives life to the person's spirit.

Romans 3:28 For we maintain that a man is justified by faith apart from works of the Law.

Romans 5:1-2 Therefore having been justified by faith, we have peace with God through our Lord Jesus Christ, through whom also we have obtained our introduction into this grace in which we stand.

Colossians 2:13-14 And when you were dead in your transgressions...He made you alive together with Him [Christ], *having forgiven us all our transgressions, having cancelled out the certificate of debt consisting of decrees against us which was hostile to us; and He has taken it out of the way, having nailed it to the cross.*

After the instantaneous and one-time event called justification, we enter the next stage of salvation –sanctification-- which is definitely NOT one-time or instantaneous! John Wesley, founder of the Methodist movement, compared justification to the birth of a person, and sanctification to the growing and maturing of the person. Sanctification is a life-long process. Sanctification is a process of being released from the power sin has over us right now in this life.   In other words, sanctification is the process of being made holy, i.e. set apart for God's use. "Being made holy" may sound uncomfortable --if you are like me "holiness" has always sounded austere-- but really it means having our character reflect God's beautiful character and having our conduct come into line with what Jesus would do. It is having the life of Jesus come forth in us. Jesus died instead of me for my justification, and now He lives instead of me for my sanctification.

Here are a few scriptures out of many we could choose that talk about sanctification:

> *1 Thessalonians 4:3-4 For this is the will of God, your sanctification; that is, that you abstain from sexual immorality; that each of you know how to possess his own body in sanctification and honor...*
>
> *Romans 12:2 And do not be conformed to this world, but be transformed by the renewing of your mind.*
>
> *Ephesians 4:1-2 ...walk in a manner worthy of the calling with which you have been called, with all humility and gentleness, with patience, showing forbearance to one another in love.*

The third part of our salvation, glorification, will one day "save" our physical bodies from the presence of sin by taking our bodies out of the world -- a future event. Glorification means the raising from the dead and transforming of our perishable bodies into imperishable bodies that are more fitted for the life to come.

> *Romans 8:23 ...even we ourselves groan within ourselves, waiting eagerly for our adoption as sons, the redemption of our body.*
>
> *2 Thessalonians 1:7, 10 ...when the Lord Jesus shall be revealed from heaven with His mighty angels in flaming*

> fire...when He comes to be glorified in His saints [all true believers] on that day...
>
> Philippians 3:20-21 ...the Lord Jesus Christ, who will transform our lowly body into conformity with His glorious body.

Differentiating between the Parts of Salvation

If we fail to differentiate between these aspects of salvation, we can easily become confused by attempting to interpret every scripture about salvation as if it's talking about justification. For instance, think about these three verses and what they say about salvation:

> Ephesians 2:8 For by grace you have been saved through faith ... it is the gift of God.
>
> Philippians 2:12 Work out your salvation with fear and trembling.
>
> Romans 13:11 For now salvation is nearer to us than when we believed.

In the first, the Apostle Paul tells us we have been saved and it sounds like it's done. But in the next, this same Paul exhorts us to "work out" our salvation with an attitude of fear and trembling about it. In the first he sounds convinced that salvation has already happened, then in the next he sounds like our salvation is very much in doubt! We become even more confused by the third passage, by the same writer, where salvation is referred to as something we are still waiting for – it hasn't happened to us yet! How can we make sense out of this?

As I interpret it, when we see "salvation" referred to as a past event or in a tense in Greek that denotes a one-time event, it is talking about justification; when we see salvation referred to as a present event or in a continuous tense, it is talking about sanctification; and when it is referred to as a future event, it is dealing with glorification. This is the general rule and there are some exceptions, but it is a good place to start. Therefore, when Ephesians 2:8 said, "by grace you have been saved," the verb 'have been saved' is in the Greek aorist tense, which is used for a one-time action (not a continuous or repeated action): so this one-time, past-tense salvation is justification. Then when Philippians 2:12 told us to "work out our salvation," the Greek verb for 'work out' is in the present imperative tense, a command to do something that involves continuous action: so this refers to a type of salvation that is an on-going process, i.e. it is speaking of sanctification. And when Romans 13:11 wrote of a salvation (as a noun, so we don't have a verb tense to work with) that has not yet arrived but is drawing nearer to us, i.e. a salvation that is coming to us in the future, it is

Our three-fold salvation

Part of Salvation	Freedom from the...	Salvation as a...	Example
Justification	Penalty of sin	Past-tense event	Ephesians 2:8
Sanctification	Power of sin	Present-tense event	Philippians 2:12
Glorification	Presence of sin	Future event	Romans 13:11

speaking of glorification, the redemption of our body.

Here are a few more scriptures to think over within this framework. When salvation is used as a verb, I've indicated the tense of the verb in Greek.

Justification

2 Timothy 1:9 who has saved [Greek aorist tense: simple action, not repeated or continuous] *us, and called us with a holy calling, not according to our works, but according to His own purpose and grace*

Titus 3:5 He saved [aorist tense] *us, not on the basis of deeds which we have done in righteousness, but according to His mercy, by the washing of regeneration and renewing by the Holy Spirit.*

1 Peter 1:3 Blessed be the God and Father of our Lord Jesus Christ, who according to His great mercy has caused [aorist] *us to be born again to a living hope through the resurrection of Jesus Christ from the dead*

Sanctification

1 Corinthians 1:18 to us who are being saved [Gr. present participle: continuous or repeated action] *it is the power of God*

2 Corinthians 2:15 For we are a fragrance of Christ to God among those who are being saved [present participle]

1 Timothy 4:16 Keep a close watch on yourself and on the teaching. Persist in this, for by so doing you will save [future tense] *both yourself and your hearers [ESV].*

(This is one of the exceptions to the rule: a future tense 'save' that does not mean glorification. From the context the meaning is that as he pays close attention and perseveres in sharing God's word (in the future), it will do its work of sanctifying the listeners (in the future).

Glorification

Romans 5:9 having now been justified by His blood [justification], *we shall be saved* [Gr. future tense] *from the wrath of God.*

Hebrews 9:28 Christ...shall appear [Gr. future tense] *a second time, ...to those who eagerly await Him, for salvation.*

1 Peter 1:5 who are protected by the power of God through faith for a salvation ready to be revealed in the last time.

All Three

1 Thessalonians 5:9 For God has not destined us for wrath, but for obtaining salvation through our Lord Jesus Christ.

An Exercise

In the next scripture (diagram below), I have circled the parts that refer to justification, sanctification, and glorification. As an exercise, if you'd like to see if you can spot them before reading on, I've left the following group unmarked:

Colossians 2:6-7 Therefore as you have received [Gr. aorist tense] *Christ Jesus the Lord, so walk* [Gr. present imperative, a command to do something with continuous or repeated action] *in Him, having been firmly rooted* [Gr. perfect participle, emphasizes the finished results of an action] *and now being built up* [Gr. present participle, continuous or repeated action] *in Him...*

Colossians 3:1-4 Therefore if you have been raised up [aorist] *with Christ, keep seeking* [present imperative] *the things above, where Christ is, seated at the right hand of God. Set* [present imperative] *your mind on the things above, not on the things that are on earth. For you have died* [aorist] *and your life is hidden* [Gr. perfect indicative, emphasizes either the perfectness of the action or the finished result] *with Christ in God. When Christ, who is our life, is revealed* [Gr. aorist subjunctive], *then you also will be revealed* [Gr. future] *with Him in glory.*

Now here are the scriptures with the three parts circled:

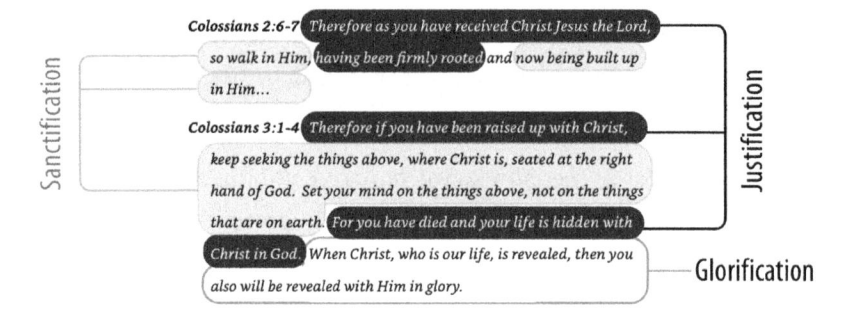

<blockquote>
Sanctification | Justification

Colossians 2:6-7 <mark>Therefore as you have received Christ Jesus the Lord,</mark> so walk in Him, <mark>having been firmly rooted</mark> and now being built up in Him...

Colossians 3:1-4 <mark>Therefore if you have been raised up with Christ,</mark> keep seeking the things above, where Christ is, seated at the right hand of God. Set your mind on the things above, not on the things that are on earth. <mark>For you have died and your life is hidden with Christ in God.</mark> When Christ, who is our life, is revealed, then you also will be revealed with Him in glory.
</blockquote>

— Glorification

Three Parts of Man with the Three Parts of Salvation

Before we leave this subject, we should take note of the connection between the three parts of man and the three parts of salvation.

It's obvious that glorification is a salvation that will happen to our bodies.

> *Romans 8:23 ...waiting eagerly for...the redemption of our body.*
>
> *Philippians 3:20-21 ...who will transform our lowly body into conformity with His glorious body.*

But then, because we tend to blur the distinction between spirit and soul, it's not as obvious that justification is a salvation that happens in a person's spirit. It is our spirit that was dead and has been made alive, born again by the Spirit of God. Spirit, Jesus said, gives birth to spirit. This new-born spirit is joined to the Spirit of Christ.

> *John 3:3, 7 Jesus answered and said to him, "Truly, truly, I say to you, unless one is born again, he cannot see the kingdom of God. ... You must be born again."*

> *John 3:6 That which is born of the flesh is flesh; and that which is born of the Spirit is spirit.*
>
> *1 Corinthians 6:17 But the one who joins himself to the Lord is one spirit with Him.* [F]
>
> *Galatians 4:6 And because you are sons, God has sent forth the Spirit of His Son into our hearts, crying, "Abba, Father!"*
>
> *Romans 8:9-10 ...But if anyone does not have the Spirit of Christ, he does not belong to Him. And if Christ is in you, though the body is dead because of sin, yet the spirit is alive because of righteousness.*

Finally, if we are careful in our use of Scripture, we'll understand that the soul is the part of man in which the salvation called sanctification takes place.

> *James 1:21 Therefore putting aside all filthiness and all that remains of wickedness, in humility receive the word implanted, which is able to save your souls.*
>
> *1 Peter 1:9 obtaining as the outcome of your faith the salvation of your souls*
>
> *Romans 12:2 And do not be conformed to this world, but be transformed by the renewing of your mind.*

Here is the best illustration I have heard that depicts our initial salvation and our on-going salvation, which I heard from a wonderful Bible teacher, Clay Hudson. Imagine that a gardener comes across an old rose trellis that is overgrown with a green briar - a very tough weed to remove. The wise gardener takes one chop at the green briar and cuts it through at ground level, meanwhile planting a small rose bush at the base of the trellis. If you just glanced at the weed, you would think it was still alive, but if you looked closely and saw that it was cut off from its roots, you'd call it dead. Gradually the rose begins to grow, and as it grows, the gardener breaks off parts of the now-drying green briar to make way for the rose. Eventually the rose takes over more and more of the trellis, and what had supported the ugliness of the green briar eventually supports the loveliness and fragrance of the rose. You see the interpretation: the green briar represents a person's old nature, the rose his new-born spirit, and the trellis his soul, through which the old or new nature will be expressed.

Our understanding is reinforced by the history of Israel: before the people of Israel came into the Promised Land, God told them that he wouldn't remove the hostile peoples all at once, but would drive them out little by little.

> *Exodus 23:29-30 I will not drive them out before you in a single year, that the land may not become desolate, and the beasts of the field become too numerous for you. I will drive them out before you little by little, until you become fruitful and take possession of the land.*

So, although justification is instantaneous and glorification will be instantaneous, sanctification is little by little!

I hope that this study has been a blessing to you and has clarified some things for you while we marvel together at God's provision to save the whole person: spirit, soul, and body.

Endnotes, Chapter 5

[F] Understanding this makes sense of the puzzling verse *1 John 3:9 "No one who is born of God practices sin, because His seed abides in him; and he cannot sin, because he is born of God."* The part of us that is born again is our spirit. Our born-again spirit is joined to the Spirit of Christ and therefore incapable of sinning.

Chapter Six
Repentance

We have seen that our initial salvation comes through repentance and faith. Repentance and faith also play large roles in our ongoing salvation. So we need to understand these concepts well. This chapter will look at repentance, and faith will be our topic for the next.

If you are like I am, you start with a negative bias toward repentance, as something that seems negative and hard. But we should think of it as we think of taking medicine or an appointment with the dentist: repentance is unpleasant for a short while, but it is the gateway to the relief for what ails us!

Before we get to the remedy, though, let's take a deeper look at the problem.

Understanding Sin

Ask a Western Christian to define sin, and you are likely to get the definition, "falling short of the glory of God," or "missing the mark, not coming into what God intended for us." This is correct as far as it goes, but if it is our total understanding, we may be missing some important elements. Let me expand on this.

In his heart-felt poem on repentance after being confronted by Nathan the prophet, David uses three Hebrew words to portray a complete description of sin:

> *Psalm 51:1-2 "Be gracious to Me, O God, according to Thy*
> *lovingkindness;*

> *According to the greatness of Thy compassion blot out my <u>transgressions</u>.*
>
> *Wash me thoroughly from my <u>iniquity</u>,*
>
> *And cleanse me from my <u>sin</u>."*

Let's start with the last word because this is the most familiar definition to most: "sin" in Hebrew is *chatha*, which means missing the way or falling short. But watch, sin is also described as "transgressions," the Hebrew word *pasha*, which means rebellion, a willful crossing of the line. Not only has my sin caused me to miss what God has for me, sin is rebellion within me! Then we add the third description, "iniquity," which is the Hebrew *avah*, to be bent or twisted, to be depraved. Sin has distorted us, it has made us deformed; specifically, I think it has made us self-absorbed, so that our own needs and desires seem paramount. Martin Luther said it this way, "Sin, so deeply curved in on itself" (*Lectures on Romans*).

If we use the analogy of an arrow, "sin" means that the arrow fell short of the target. But if that's our total definition, we might conclude that it's not the arrow's fault! If an arrow is not launched with enough force to go as far as the target, is that the arrow's fault? It could be the fault of the bow that launched the arrow, so the poor arrow just didn't have enough energy behind it! But then we add "rebellion" to our definition, and understand that the arrow fell short because it did not <u>want</u> to hit the target, in fact this arrow would rather land anywhere <u>but</u> the target. The arrow actually chose to fall short, it wants to avoid the target because it is rebellious. (A parent told the story of taking their three-year-old to a basketball game, and clearly showing the child the boundary line of the playing court, and telling the toddler not to go across that line, that he could go anywhere else but across the line, explaining that it is dangerous over there, players are running around and the child could get hurt. Of course you know what happened next!

After a few minutes, the child walked up to the line, looked back at the parents sitting in the stands, and put one foot across the line. That's our human nature, deliberately crossing the line in defiance of the rule!) Finally, if we add "being twisted" to our definition, we see that the arrow fell short because it was a twisted, selfish arrow, intent on hitting another target, the target of its own ambition. A twisted, selfish, rebellious arrow did not hit the mark.

Let's see what else Luther has to say about sin, which sounds so modern!

> "It enjoys itself and uses everyone else, even God; it seeks itself and its own interests in everything: it brings it about that man is finally and ultimately concerned only for himself. This is the idolatry that determines all he does, feels, undertakes, thinks, and speaks. Good is only what is good for him and bad only what is bad for him" (*Luther's Commentary on Romans 8*).

Repercussions of Sin in Human Nature

Notice the three immediate repercussions sinning had in Adam and Eve: shame, fear, and guilt.

> *Genesis 3:6-13 When the woman saw that the tree was good for food, and that it was a delight to the eyes, and that the tree was desirable to make one wise, she took from its fruit and ate; and she gave also to her husband with her, and he ate. Then the eyes of both of them were opened, and they knew that they were naked; and they sewed fig leaves together and made themselves loin coverings. And they heard the sound of the LORD God walking in the garden in the cool of the day, and the man and his wife hid themselves from the presence of the LORD God among the trees of the garden. Then the LORD God called to the man, and said to him, "Where are you?" And he said, "I heard the sound of Thee in the*

garden, and I was afraid because I was naked; so I hid myself." And He said, "Who told you that you were naked? Have you eaten from the tree of which I commanded you not to eat?"

The first emotion they experienced after eating the fruit was shame about their nakedness, which they tried to solve by sewing leaves together and covering themselves. Then next, when they heard God coming near, they were afraid and hid from God, not wanting to face Him. Finally they were confronted with their guilt of transgressing the command with God's words, "Have you...?"

All of us experience these psychological effects of sin. Shame makes us feel dirty and we want to have our shame removed or at least covered over. Fear makes us secretive and seeking for control; we want power so we can ensure that the event that made us fearful will not happen again. And guilt hangs a dread of coming punishment over us; we try to do good works or be perfect to make up for the acts we feel guilty about.

Further, depending on the culture into which we were born, one of these reactions is felt more keenly than the other two. Through the centuries these initial reactions have embedded themselves into the three basic groupings of cultures and religions we see today: shame-based (the Islamic world, India, Japan), fear-based (Africa and the Amazon basin), and guilt-based (Europe and the Americas, Western culture).

Repentance is the Gateway to Forgiveness

Notice how these scriptures link repentance to forgiveness: Acts 5:31 "to grant repentance to Israel, and forgiveness of sins," and Luke 24:47 "that repentance for forgiveness of sins should be proclaimed in His name."

How does the Bible define repentance? Repentance is:

Turning: *Acts 26:18 "To open their eyes so that they may turn from darkness to light and from the dominion of Satan to God, in order that they may receive forgiveness of sins."*

Returning: *Acts 3:19 "Repent therefore and return, that your sins may be wiped away, in order that times of refreshing may come from the presence of the Lord."*

Forsaking: *Isaiah 55:7 "Let the wicked forsake his way, and the unrighteous man his thoughts; and let him return to the Lord, and He will have compassion on him; and to our God, for He will abundantly pardon."*

What wonderful relief repentance brings! It's the gateway to light instead of darkness, to living under God's control instead of Satan's, to having our sins wiped away, and to times that are spiritually refreshing. The literal, most simple meaning of repent is "think again", "changing one's mind or purpose." (*Vine's Expository Dictionary of New Testament Words*). We have inherited a nature and lifestyle but we don't have to continue in it, we can rethink it! If we find ourselves trapped by destructive habits or plagued by unwelcome thoughts, there is a way out!

"Come now, and let us reason together," says the Lord,
"though your sins are as scarlet [an indelible dye], *they will be as white as snow" (Isaiah 1:18).*

The famous preacher, Charles Spurgeon, defined repentance is "a heart broken for sin and from sin... It is a change of mind of the most thorough kind, and has in it sorrow for the past and a resolve for change in the future."

Three Elements of Repentance:
Acknowledging, Sorrowing, and Forsaking

Before we can do anything about sin we first must become aware of it, and admit to God that it exists.

> *Proverbs 28:13 He who conceals his transgressions will not prosper, but he who confesses...will find compassion.*

Our natural tendency is to try to hide our sin or live in denial, but this will get us nowhere in the spiritual life. We must take responsibility for what we have done wrong. If we will, we can find relief.

The next element of a true attitude of repentance is what the Bible calls "godly sorrow." In general, people have a shallow understanding of what repentance is and what it costs. They think that to simply say, "I'm sorry," is enough and should make everything right. But we'll see in the next scripture that true repentance goes far beyond just saying that we're sorry.

> *2 Corinthians 7:9-11 I now rejoice, not that you were made sorrowful, but that you were made sorrowful to the point of repentance; for you were made sorrowful according to the will of God, in order that you might not suffer loss in anything through us. For the sorrow that is according to the will of God produces a repentance without regret, leading to salvation; but the sorrow of the world produces death. For behold what earnestness this very thing, this godly sorrow, has produced in you: what vindication of yourselves, what indignation, what fear, what longing, what zeal, what avenging of wrong!*

I once took a boy home to his father who had been caught shoplifting, and the first words out of his father's mouth were, "Why did you get caught?!" His father communicated quite clearly that he was upset with his son not so much for stealing, but for being careless enough to get caught stealing. In this case, shame on the family was stronger than guilt. Verse 9 makes clear that it's possible to be sorry without repenting. Being sorry by itself is not repentance. Sometimes we're sorry that we got caught, but not so sorry for what we did. We haven't recognized how our sin has offended God or hurt people. These verses tell us that what the Bible calls "godly sorrow" contains:

- vindication (absolving anyone who was falsely accused),

- fear (of continuing to offend),

- longing (wishing that it had never happened),

- zeal (for right), and

- avenging of wrong (putting right anything we can, to undo the effect of the wrong act). A true attitude of repentance wants to restore or make right the damage caused by what was done wrong.

How far short a mere "I'm sorry" is from real repentance!

Repentance involves forsaking the behaviors or thoughts, i.e. leaving them behind.

> *Proverbs 28:13 "He who conceals his transgressions will not prosper, but he who confesses and forsakes them will find compassion."*

> *Matthew 3:8 "Therefore bring forth fruit in keeping with repentance."*

How to Repent Successfully

We can look at some famous opportunities to repent in the Bible and learn from others – mostly from their mistakes – how to repent successfully.

1) Don't try to hide your sin, like Cain.

> *Genesis 4:8-10 And it came about when they were in the field, that Cain rose up against Abel his brother and killed him. Then the Lord said to Cain, "Where is Abel your brother?" And he said, "I do not know. Am I my brother's keeper?" And He said, "What have you done? The voice of your brother's blood is crying to Me from the ground."*

What Cain did not know was that "nothing in all creation is hidden from God's sight. Everything is uncovered and laid bare before the eyes of him to whom we must give account" (Hebrews 4:13).

2) Don't try to shift the blame to someone else, as the story of Adam and Eve.

> *Genesis 3:11-13 And He said, "Who told you that you were naked? Have you eaten from the tree of which I commanded you not to eat?" And the man said, "The woman whom Thou gave to be with me, she gave me from the tree, and I ate." Then the Lord God said to the woman, "What is this you have done?" And the woman said, "The serpent deceived me, and I ate."*

The very first words out of Adam's mouth when God questions him are, "the woman." (Men have been blaming women ever since!) Adam even tries to throw some of the blame on God by saying, "The woman You gave me." So next, God turned to Eve. Did she do any better? Her first words were, "The serpent." She in turn was saying, 'It's not my fault, the devil made me do it!' These were the first attempts at blame-shifting, but they would not be the last!

3) Don't try to minimize the seriousness of your sin is, as King Saul tried to do.

> *1 Samuel 15:13-30 And Samuel came to Saul, and Saul said to him, "Blessed are you of the Lord! I have carried out the command of the Lord." But Samuel said, "What then is this bleating of the sheep in my ears, and the lowing of the oxen which I hear?" And Saul said, "They have brought them from the Amalekites, for the people spared the best of the sheep and oxen, to sacrifice to the Lord your God; but the rest we have utterly destroyed... (verse 21) but the people took some of the spoil, sheep and oxen, the choicest of the things devoted to destruction, to sacrifice to the Lord your God at Gilgal."*

> *And Samuel said, "Has the Lord as much delight in burnt offerings and sacrifices as in obeying the voice of the Lord? Behold, to obey is better than sacrifice, and to heed than the fat of rams. For rebellion is as the sin of divination, and insubordination is as iniquity and idolatry. Because you have rejected the word of the Lord, He has also rejected you from being king." Then Saul said to Samuel, "I have sinned; I have indeed transgressed the command of the Lord and your words, because I feared the people and listened to their voice. Now therefore, please pardon my sin and return with me, that I may worship the Lord." ... (verse 30) Then he said, "I have sinned; but please honor me now before the elders of my people and before Israel, and go back with me, that I may worship the Lord your God."*

Notice where King Saul places his own behavior. In verse 15 he says, "for <u>the people</u> spared the best of the sheep and oxen, to sacrifice to the Lord your God; but the rest <u>we</u> have utterly destroyed." And in verse 21, "But <u>the people</u> took some of the spoil." His attitude was that it was the people's fault, not his. When he finally admits his transgression, he regards it so lightly that he can say in verse 30, "I have sinned, but please honor me now." Someone who truly feels the shame of his conduct does not, in the next breath, set conditions on how he should be treated.

4) If possible, make restitution, like Zaccheus.

> *Luke 19:5-10 And when Jesus came to the place, He looked up and said to him, "Zaccheus, hurry and come down, for today I must stay at your house." And he hurried and came down, and received Him gladly. And when they saw it, they all began to grumble, saying, "He has gone to be the guest of a man who is a sinner." And Zaccheus stopped and said to the Lord, "Behold, Lord, half of my possessions I will give to the poor, and if I*

> have defrauded anyone of anything, I will give back four times as much." And Jesus said to him, "Today salvation has come to this house, because he, too, is a son of Abraham. For the Son of Man has come to seek and to save that which was lost."

When Zaccheus offered to pay back four times the amount of the money he had gotten dishonestly, he was doing what the Law required (see Exodus 22:1). This gesture by itself shows his true change of heart and his desire to make restitution where he had caused hurt. But he goes even further by promising to give away half of his wealth to the poor.

Repentance Affects the Penalty for Sin, but not Always the Consequences

King David's experience of sin and recovery brings out one other point that is critical to our understanding of repentance, which highlights the difference between the guilt of sin and the consequences of sin. As we pick up the story, David had committed adultery with the wife of one of his leaders, named Uriah, and then conspired to kill Uriah so the adultery would not become known. A year had passed without discovery of David's sins when the passage begins.

> *2 Samuel 12:7-15 Nathan then said to David, "You are the man! Thus says the Lord God of Israel, 'It is I who anointed you king over Israel and it is I who delivered you from the hand of Saul. I also gave you your master's house and your master's wives into your care, and I gave you the house of Israel and Judah; and if that had been too little, I would have added to you many more things like these! Why have you despised the word of the Lord by doing evil in His sight? You have struck down Uriah the Hittite with the sword, have taken his wife to be your wife, and have killed him with the sword of the sons of Ammon. Now therefore, the sword shall never*

> *depart from your house, because you have despised Me and have taken the wife of Uriah the Hittite to be your wife.' Thus says the Lord, 'Behold, I will raise up evil against you from your own household; I will even take your wives before your eyes, and give them to your companion, and he shall lie with your wives in broad daylight. Indeed you did it secretly, but I will do this thing before all Israel, and under the sun.'" Then David said to Nathan, "I have sinned against the Lord." And Nathan said to David, "The Lord also has taken away your sin; you shall not die. However, because by this deed you have given occasion to the enemies of the Lord to blaspheme, the child also that is born to you shall surely die." So Nathan went to his house. Then the Lord struck the child that Uriah's widow bore to David, so that he was very sick.*

David repents beautifully. He simply says, "I have sinned against the Lord," without any blame-shifting or equivocating. He took full responsibility for his actions and offered no excuses. Sometimes, the less said, the better. Immediately on the heels of his repentance God grants a "presidential pardon" to him (v.13), announcing that David would not die. However, because the Gentile nations could easily misunderstand God's nature if God did nothing, the prophet predicted that the child would die and David would experience certain conflicts in the future. As his history unfolded, David's last twenty years were twenty years of family strife and violence, all of which had been set in motion by his sin. His daughter Tamar was raped by her half-brother Amnon, then Tamar's full brother Absalom took revenge and killed Amnon. Absalom fled from David because of the murder, and later returned - and David did nothing. (He probably thought, how can I punish Absalom when I have done worse? Yet as the king and main court of justice of the land he should have taken action.) Absalom grew to despise David, won the hearts of the people with "if I were king" speeches, and eventually led an armed rebellion against his father.

All this happened as a consequence of sin; it had been set in motion by David's one night of passion with Bathsheba. Was the passion pleasant? We imagine so. Was it worth twenty years of suffering? Hardly.

David's experience illuminates the difference between guilt and consequences. His guilt was forgiven by God when he repented; therefore, I have to conclude that in heaven David had nothing to answer for regarding this sin. But that did not erase the consequences. His sin had set certain things in motion that had to be played out.

How can we illustrate this difference between guilt and consequences? Imagine you are on a steep hillside and see someone below you on the hill that you hate. In a sudden flash of anger you roll a stone at him. The stone dislodges other stones and soon a rockslide is gaining momentum down the hillside. At this point you come to your senses and cry out, "God forgive me!" You feel horror over what you did. You wish you hadn't done it and would give anything to turn time back ten seconds. Will God forgive you? Yes, God will forgive -- but the rocks continue to slide! Sometimes in God's mercy the "rocks" miss the person below, but often they don't. Even after the sin is forgiven, we may have to live with its consequences.

This story is fictitious, but you can apply its principle to any number of behaviors that are all too real. Can a murderer be forgiven? Certainly. But it will not bring his victim back to life or erase the pain of the families affected. Can a drunkard be rehabilitated and changed by the power of God? Of course! But it won't restore the time he lost with his children or the psychological damage they suffered.

So, sin incurs not only guilt but also consequences. The New Testament talks about the consequences of sin when it says, "Do not be deceived: God cannot be mocked. A man reaps what he sows" (Galatians 6:7, NIV). Here's the law of sowing and reaping in a nutshell: we reap what we sow, at a later time than we sow, in a greater quantity than we sowed. When we think about sin, we need to remember that our actions are continually sowing for good or ill. Whatever we plant is coming back to us!

Excerpts from *The Believer's New Life* by Andrew Murray (Bethany House 1984, pp.48-50.)

> The only counsel concerning sin is to bring it immediately to the only One who can take it away--God himself. You should learn that one of the greatest privileges of a child of God is the confession of sin; through confession I hand over my sin to God, lay it down on God, renounce it before God, cast it into the fiery oven of God's holy love... Many believers fail to understand this. There is a general tendency to try to cover sin, or to make it less...
>
> Let your confession be a definite one. The continued vague confession of sin does more harm than good. It is much better to say to God that you have nothing to confess than to try to confess what you do not know. Begin with one sin. Let it come to a complete harmony between God and you concerning this one sin. Let it be fixed with you that this sin, through confession, is placed in God's hands. You will experience that in true confession there is both power and blessing.
>
> Let the confession be a truthful one... Give up your sin that God may forgive you and cleanse you from it. Do not confess sin if you are not prepared, if you do not heartily desire to be freed from it.

Let confession be trustful. Put your confidence in God actually forgiving you and also cleansing you from sin.

New believer, do you understand it now? What must you do with sin, with every sin? Bring it in confession to God; give it to God. God alone takes away sin."

Chapter Seven
Faith

What Faith Is and Is Not

As we begin our examination of this vital subject, let's start by understanding what faith is not.

First, faith does not depend on "sight," i.e. the evidence of our natural senses.

2 Corinthians 5:7 For we walk by faith, and not by sight.

The world-system says, "Seeing is believing," but St. Augustine expressed the attitude of faith when he said, "Faith is to believe what we do not see, and the reward of this faith is to see what we believe." (*Great Lives, Great Deeds*, Readers Digest 1964, p.213.)

> *John 5:5-9 And a certain man was there, who had been thirty-eight years in his sickness. When Jesus saw him lying there, and knew that he had already been a long time in that condition, He said to him, "Do you wish to get well?" The sick man answered Him, "Sir, I have no man to put me into the pool when the water is stirred up, but while I am coming, another steps down before me." Jesus said to him, "Arise, take up your pallet, and walk." And immediately the man became well, and took up his pallet and began to walk.*

When Jesus told the paralytic to rise and walk, the sick man could have responded, 'Well, sir, that is just the problem, you see. I can't walk, and I haven't been able to for 38 years. You're asking me to do the one thing I can't do!' All the evidence of his senses, backed by his years of experience, was telling the man he couldn't walk. But his faith responded to something different than his natural senses, and he was healed.

Faith also doesn't depend on our feelings.

1 John 3:19-20 We shall know by this that we are of the truth, and shall assure our heart before Him, in whatever our heart condemns us; for God is greater than our heart and knows all things.

We put our faith in the facts of God's word, not in our feelings. If we let ourselves be led by our feelings, we will be misled. Our faith needs to be based firmly on what God says is true, not on what we "feel" inside.

Faith is more than hope.

Hebrews 11:1 Faith is the assurance of things hoped for.

Hope is related to faith, but faith goes beyond just hoping for something; faith includes an assurance that what is hoped for will come into being. Often we pray prayers that are more prayers of hope than prayers of faith; our praying never gets beyond the hoping stage into real

> **Faith is not sight, feeling, or mere hope.**

faith. Then we wonder why our prayers weren't answered.

The Bible has a lot to say about faith, but the only definition is what we just read in Hebrews 11:1, "Faith is the assurance of things hoped for, the conviction of things not seen." Faith is convinced of the reality of things that can't be seen or perceived with the natural senses. Faith is sure about something God has promised. Therefore, faith has to be firmly rooted in what God has said. Abraham demonstrated his faith for us as his and Sarah's bodies got too old to have children, yet God had promised them a son. Romans 4:20-21 tells us what was happening inside Abraham: "yet, with respect to the promise of God, he did not waver in unbelief, but grew strong in faith, giving glory to God, and being fully assured that what He had promised, He was able also to perform." Faith looks at God's promises and is sure that He will fulfill them, even in spite of circumstances to the contrary.

> *Mark 10:15 Truly I say to you, whoever does not receive the kingdom of God like a child shall not enter it at all.*

Faith is not complicated because even children can have faith. Our faith needs to be child-like. In Greek, to "believe" simply means to trust in and rely on.

> "What is faith? None other than the certainty that what God says is true. When God says that something shall come to pass, or that He will do something for me, this is for faith just as good as if I had seen it." (Andrew Murray, *The Believer's New Life*, Bethany House 1984, p.26)

> "The faith that the Bible speaks of is not antithetical to reason. ...Faith in the biblical sense is substantive, based on the knowledge that the One in whom that faith is placed has proven that He is worthy of that trust. In its essence, faith is a confidence in the person of Jesus Christ and in His power, so that even when His power does not serve my end, my confidence in Him remains because of who He is." (Ravi Zacharias, *Jesus Among Other Gods*, Word Publishing 2000, p.58.)

I had a dramatic encounter with faith when I was a university student. I had been sharing the gospel with another student named Phyllis, who couldn't seem to understand at all what I was saying to her. One evening as I was studying at my desk, the thought suddenly came to me, "Claim Phyllis [for salvation]!" The instant God spoke to my heart, a great certainty also came to me that Phyllis would be saved. I knew it for sure. I got very excited, jumped up from my chair, and paced around the room praying for Phyllis to be saved. I just knew it would happen.

But nothing happened in Phyllis for a long time. After graduation, she worked in a grocery store and sometimes I would see her there. I remember asking more than once, "Are you saved yet?" and her reply, "No, not yet." Then I would say, "Well, don't worry, you will be!" Five years passed and Phyllis still was not saved. Then one day the phone rang and Phyllis wanted to talk because she was troubled about eternity. And guess what? Phyllis committed her life to Jesus. That was thirty-five years ago, and today Phyllis continues to walk with the Lord.

We also need to understand that faith is not presumption; faith starts with a word from God we have heard. Romans 10:17 "So faith comes from hearing, and hearing by the word of Christ." Faith is not some magic formula or genie lamp that we can rub and make all our wishes come true. God is the initiator of faith, and if we get ahead of Him, we'll get into trouble. Faith responds to God's word to us, often to a

> **Faith is not presumption.**

specific word about a specific situation.

Having told a success story about faith, let me tell another from the same year of university studies, in which my attempt to have faith was unsuccessful. I was studying what the Bible said about physical healing, and saw general promises of healing, which I began to apply to the fact that I wore eyeglasses. If God heals, why was I wearing glasses? I had no specific word or "quickening" to my heart concerning God healing my eyesight (as I had when God spoke to me about Phyllis' salvation), but I thought that if I "moved in faith" it would cause the miracle to happen, that the healing was mine and any symptoms to the contrary were lies. If I acted as if I didn't need glasses, and told people I was healed, my eyesight would become 20/20, I thought. I made the mistake of moving in presumption, taking action without a specific word from Christ. So this is what I did: I broke my glasses and threw them in the trash, flicked my contact lenses out of the window, and told people God had healed me and I was only waiting for the manifestation of the healing. Then I lived for the next six months without seeing well, because my vision is 20/200 – I see at 20 feet what perfect eyes would see at 200 feet! During this time I was even enrolled in an art history course, viewing pictures projected onto a screen in front of the class. Of course I wouldn't sit right up front, because that would be admitting that my eyes weren't healed. So I had fallen into the name-it-and-you-have-it teaching before I heard it taught by anyone. All that was missing was a word from the Lord, and any assurance in my heart that I really had been healed. Finally I went back to the eye doctor, and now I see well – with my glasses.

If I had been healed with this poor understanding of how faith operates, I might have been in danger of making a savior of my faith. Listen to what Charles Spurgeon had to say about this.

> "Still, I remind you that faith is only the channel or aqueduct, and not the fountainhead, and we must not look so much to it that we exalt it above the divine source of all blessing which lies in the grace of God. Never make a Christ out of your faith, nor think of as if it were the independent source of your salvation. Our life is found in 'looking unto Jesus' (Hebrews 12:2), not in looking to our own faith. By faith all things become possible to us, yet the power is not in the faith but in the God upon whom faith relies." (C.H. Spurgeon, *All of Grace*, Moody Press, pp. 43-44.)

Faith Changes Things, Inside and Out

Hebrews 11 is the great chapter about the heroes of faith. Notice the outward things that changed because of the action of faith:

Hebrews 11:29-34 By faith they passed through the Red Sea as though they were passing through dry land; and the Egyptians, when they attempted it, were drowned. By faith the walls of Jericho fell down, after they had been encircled for seven days. By faith Rahab the harlot did not perish along with those who were disobedient, after she had welcomed the spies in peace. And what more shall I say? For time will fail me if I tell of Gideon, Barak, Samson, Jephthah; of David and Samuel and the prophets; who by faith conquered kingdoms, performed acts of righteousness, obtained promises, shut the mouths of lions, quenched the power of fire, escaped the edge of the sword, from weakness were made strong, became mighty in war, put foreign armies to flight.

And now let's see what changed inwardly in Moses because of his faith:

Hebrews 11:24-27 By faith Moses, when he had grown up, refused to be called the son of Pharaoh's daughter; choosing rather to endure ill-treatment with the people of God, than to enjoy the passing pleasures of sin; considering the reproach of Christ greater riches than the treasures of Egypt; for he was looking to the reward.

Moses chose ill treatment rather than pleasure, and considered reproach to be better than riches, because of his faith. A person with real faith will act differently than a person without faith. If we really have faith, it will find a way to show itself in good works. Martin Luther said it best when he said, "Good works do not make a good man, but a good man does good works" ("*On Christian Liberty*").

> *James 2:14-16 What use is it, my brethren, if a man says he has faith, but he has no works? Can that faith save him? If a brother or sister is without clothing and in need of daily food, and one of you says to them, "Go in peace, be warmed and be filled," and yet you do not give them what is necessary for their body, what use is that? Even so faith, if it has no works, is dead, being by itself.*
>
> *Titus 2:11-14 For the grace of God has appeared, bringing salvation to all men, instructing us to deny ungodliness and worldly desires and to live sensibly, righteously and godly in the present age, looking for the blessed hope and the appearing of the glory of our great God and Savior, Christ Jesus; who gave Himself for us, that He might redeem us from every lawless deed and purify for Himself a people for His own possession, zealous for good deeds.*

Let's ask Andrew Murray to add his advice to what we've been learning about faith.

> "Blessed is she that believed; for there shall be a performance of those things which were told her from the Lord" (Luke 1:45). "I believe God, that it shall be even as it was told me" (Acts 27:25). "[Abraham] was strong in faith,…being fully persuaded that, what he had promised, he was able also to perform" (Rom.4:20,21).
>
> Let me ask my reader to read over once again the three verses which stand above, and to find out what is the primary thought they teach about faith. Read nothing into them, but simply read these words of God and ask yourself what they teach you about faith.
>
> They help us see that faith always attaches itself to what God has said or promised. When an honorable man says anything, he also does it; back of the saying follows

the doing. So also it is with God: when He would do anything, He says so first in His Word. ... Before I ever feel or experience anything, I hold fast the promise; and I know by faith that God will make it good to me.

What is faith? None other than the certainty that what God says is true... Faith always asks only for what God has said, and then relies on His faithfulness and power to fulfill His Word.

Let us now review again the words of Scripture. Of Mary we read: "Blessed is she that believed; for there shall be a performance of the things which were told her from the Lord." All things that have been spoken in the Word shall be fulfilled for me; so I believe them. Of Abraham it is reported that he was fully assured that that which had been promised, God was also able to fulfill. This is assurance of faith--to be assured that God will do what He has promised. This is precisely stated in the words of Paul: "I believe God, that it shall be even as it was told me."

New believers in Christ, the new, the eternal life that is in you, is a life of faith. And do you not see how simple and how blessed this life of faith is? I go daily to the Word and hear what God has said that He has done and will do. I take time to store in my heart the word which God says; and I hold it fast, completely certain that what God has promised, He is able to perform. And then in a childlike spirit I wait for the fulfillment of all the glorious promises of His Word. God promises; I believe; God fulfills: that is the secret of the new life.

(Andrew Murray, *The Believer's New Life*, Bethany House 1984, pp.25-27.)

Chapter Eight
Water Baptism

As soon as the subject of water baptism comes up, we are confronted with the fact that different churches and denominations have practices that vary significantly from each. And the various interpretations of baptism are so different that they cannot all be correct! I can only suggest that 1) we recognize that we have emotional attachments to our own traditions that make objectivity difficult, and 2) we try to put aside our own traditions for a moment and examine this topic by looking at what the scripture says by itself. I hope our study will lead us to see how beautiful and meaningful this sacrament is, but also how misunderstood.

It may help us right at the start, to realize that the English word "baptize" is not a translation but a transliteration, that is, a foreign word that has been adopted into our language without giving us its meaning. English is adept at absorbing foreign words and making them part of the language. For instance, we transliterate the Arabic *Qur'an* into "Koran" (changing the pronunciation slightly), while a translation of *Qur'an* would read, "The Recitation." From French we get "sabotage" and understand its meaning, but miss the history lesson of a literal translation: "*sabot*" is French for "shoe" and "*sabotage*" means "throwing in the shoe," which came from the days when French peasants would express their protests by throwing their wooden shoes into machinery to break it.

By this process of transliteration, *baptizo* became "baptize," and its meaning became partially obscured. According to Vine's Expository

Dictionary of New Testament Words, the Greek *baptizo* means simply "to dip." It was a word in use for dyeing a garment -- cloth was "baptized" into dye by dipping it and taking it out again -- or for dipping one vessel into another to draw water. ^G

Water Baptism Is a Response to the Good News

As we read the next scriptures, we will see that the early church presented water baptism as a way for a sinner to respond to the gospel. Read these as if you had never heard the first thing about water baptism and see what you conclude.

> *Acts 2:37-38 Now when they heard this, they were pierced to the heart, and said to Peter and the rest of the apostles, "Brethren, what shall we do?" And Peter said to them, "Repent, and let each of you be baptized in the name of Jesus Christ for the forgiveness of your sins..."*

> *Acts 9:17-19 And Ananias departed and entered the house, and after laying his hands on him said, "Brother Saul, the Lord Jesus, who appeared to you on the road by which you were coming, has sent me so that you may regain your sight, and be filled with the Holy Spirit." And immediately there fell from his eyes something like scales, and he regained his sight, and he arose and was baptized; and he took food and was strengthened.*

> *Acts 16:29-34 And he called for lights and rushed in and, trembling with fear, he fell down before Paul and Silas, and after he brought them out, he said, "Sirs, what must I do to be saved?" And they said, "Believe in the Lord Jesus, and you shall be saved, you and your household." And they spoke the word of the Lord to him together with all who were in his house. And he took them that very hour of the night and washed their wounds, and immediately he was baptized, he and all his household.*

As I read these passages, the first thing that stands out to me is that water baptism seems to be the "altar call" of the early Christians. We could say that it is the most scriptural way to respond to the gospel. In the early Church, we see water baptism being presented as the way a sinner should show his repentance upon hearing the gospel. Today we are more likely to ask someone to respond by coming up the aisle, praying the sinners' prayer, etc., but in scripture we see an invitation to be baptized.

At the same time, the apostles had no misunderstanding about the requirements for salvation. To the Philippian jailer's magnificent question, "What must I do to be saved?" Paul answers with a straightforward "Believe in the Lord Jesus" without mentioning baptism or any other work. In another place Paul said, "For Christ did not send me to baptize, but to preach the gospel" (1 Corinthians 1:17); how could he say such a thing if baptism was necessary for salvation? (More about this in Appendix A.)

The next surprise, when compared to our modern practices, is the sense of urgency that the early Christians had about baptizing the new convert. In fact, the three days Paul waited between his conversion on the road to Damascus and his baptism are the longest pause between conversion and baptism of anyone in the book of Acts! Check it out, here are all the other occurrences of water baptism in Acts: Acts 8:12; Acts 8:35-38; Acts 10:44-48; Acts 16:13-15. This makes me wonder what we have lost, and what are we missing, that most of us now have such a laid-back approach to baptism? Few churches baptize someone the day they get saved; most even require a waiting period (to prove the conversion is real), or attendance in a communicants' class (so they understand what they are doing), or at least to wait until it's convenient with the pastor's schedule! But these attitudes contrast sharply with the apostles'. It certainly wasn't convenient for Paul and Silas, after a long day in which they had been beaten and thrown in jail, to baptize the jailer and his family, yet they went out in the middle of the night and performed the baptisms. When was the last midnight baptism you attended? I've never been to one! What if Paul had said, "Wait until the church picnic in the summer"?

When I was a campus minister and a university student made a decision to follow Jesus, we often baptized him or her that very day. After the student had prayed for salvation, we would next explain water baptism to him and say, "Okay, let's gather up some of your friends and go to the river." We would call some church members for transportation to the river for all the college students, and then conducted the baptism right out in the open where everyone could see. It was a great way for the new Christian to start his walk with the Lord, with an open profession of his new faith! No one has ever told me that he or she regretted being baptized this way.

Water Baptism Is a Burial Service for the Old Nature

Water baptism is a way to respond to the gospel, and it is also a burial service.

> *Romans 6:3-4 Or do you not know that all of us who have been baptized into Christ Jesus have been baptized into His death? Therefore we have been buried with Him through baptism into death.*

Be careful as you read this! Did you notice that two baptisms are being discussed, or did you lump them both into one? (We are so programmed to think of water when we see the word "baptism" that it takes a paradigm shift to realize that baptism isn't always referring to water. [H]) In this passage, the first baptism mentioned is not into water but into Christ: "all of us who have been baptized <u>into Christ</u>." We are baptized into Christ when we are converted. The verse goes on to tell us something that happened automatically with this experience, that when a person is dipped into Christ, he is also dipped into Christ's death, meaning that his old nature also died at that time.

The second sentence goes on to talk of a baptism which is a burial. The conjunction "therefore" alerts us that what is spoken of next is a consequence of what came before. Since the old nature died when we believed in Jesus, "therefore" it is proper to bury it. (It would not be proper to bury something not dead, but it is totally appropriate to bury the dead!) The burial is water baptism. In water baptism we are acknowledging that our old sinful nature died with Christ on the cross. Water baptism is a burial service for the old nature. Here's another verse showing water baptism as a burial:

Colossians 2:12 having been buried with Him in baptism, in which you were also raised up with Him through faith in the working of God, who raised Him from the dead.

By going under the water we demonstrate for anyone watching that we died with Christ, and by coming up from the water we demonstrate that we have been raised with Him to a new life! So water baptism celebrates the death of the old life and the birth of the new life we have in Jesus.

Water Baptism is More than a Ceremony

When you think of water baptism, do you think of it as merely a ceremony, or does a spiritual transaction take place during baptism? In other words, does something really happen inside a person when they are baptized, or is it just a symbolic ritual?

The next verses tell us that something really happens to us when we are baptized, namely that in our soul a new separation from the world takes place.

1 Peter 3:20-21 ...in the days of Noah, during the construction of the ark, in which a few, that is, eight persons, were brought safely through the water. And

> *corresponding to that, baptism now saves you--not the removal of dirt from the flesh, but an appeal to God for a good conscience--through the resurrection of Jesus Christ.*

"Baptism now saves you," it says. As we pay attention to the tense of the verb, we notice that this is a present-tense "saves," emphasized with "now" in front of it. In Greek it is the present indicative tense, which asserts something that is occurring while the speaker is making the statement. Therefore, it is not referring to justification but to our on-going, present salvation called sanctification. By using the present tense, Peter is telling us that water baptism does something in us that is part of sanctification. What might this be, specifically?

"Corresponding to that [Noah's experience] baptism now saves you," Peter says, comparing the water of Noah's flood to the water of baptism. The water of Noah's day "saved" his family from the sinfulness of the world by lifting them above a corrupt world-system and <u>making a separation</u> between them and it. They entered into the ark (a picture of salvation in Jesus) and the water (picturing water baptism) lifted them away from the world. Thus baptism makes a separation between the believer and the influence of the world, so that its pull on the believer is weakened.

I'm reminded of a college student who came to me to be baptized after her first year at the university. She had been a Christian for a long time, but had put off being baptized. She confided to me that during freshman year she was very attracted to the weekend drinking parties. I saw her again a few months into her second year, and she said to me, "I went to a couple parties this fall, but they were boring and monotonous – the same thing week after week – and I found myself thinking, 'When are these people ever going to grow up?'" As far as I could tell, the change wasn't in the parties but in the person, because her baptism had done its work of making a distance between her and the world.

> *1 Corinthians 10:1-2 "Our fathers were all under the cloud, and all passed thru the sea; and all were baptized into Moses in the cloud and in the sea."*

Again the metaphor is repeated: with the sea on both sides and a cloud of water vapor above, water baptism is being pictured. This "baptism" made a separation between the Israelites and the power of Pharaoh. If we look for a moment at the fuller typology that the Israelites acted out, we see that in their history they were acting out stages of the Christian life. [I] They were "saved" (not literally, but as a physical picture acting out spiritual truths) through the sacrifice of the Passover lamb: we already learned that God's wrath against sin "passed over" them because of the blood of a lamb sprinkled outside their doors. This part completed the picture of justification. Next they moved on to a picture of sanctification: they began to leave Egypt (the world) and the power of Pharaoh (Satan), but soon found that the old masters didn't give up so easily. Pharaoh's army was pursuing to take them into captivity again! Isn't this exactly the experience of many young Christians? They resolve to live differently and experience for a short while a deliverance from old habits. But before long they feel the pursuit of the old lifestyle, and old friends, to drag them back into slavery. What's the answer? Should we tell them to try harder, or maybe send them to counseling? I'm all for counseling when it is needed, but let's get first things first. The answer acted out by the Israelites is water baptism! They went through the water to the other side of the Red Sea, and when the water closed after them it made a distance between them and Egypt. [J]

Water Baptism Is a Declaration to the World that This Person Has Eternal Life

> *1 John 5:8, 11 For there are three that bear witness, the Spirit and the water and the blood, and the three are one. ... (verse 11) And the witness is this, that God has given us eternal life, and this life is in His Son.*

Three witnesses. Imagine a courtroom in which you are on trial for your life – your eternal life, that is. The question of your eternal life is being decided. The prosecution claims that you do not have eternal life, but the defense says you do. The defense counsel calls three witnesses, who are "one" in their testimony – all will give evidence that you do indeed have eternal life. The three are the Holy Spirit, the water of water baptism, and the blood of Christ. Two of them are actually exhibits. For Exhibit A, the defense gives the judge those spiritual eyeglasses we mentioned earlier, by which he can see into your inner person, and with these the judge can see the blood of Jesus which was sprinkled on your heart. As Exhibit B the defense plays a video recording of your baptism, further confirmation that you are born again. Finally the defense calls the Holy Spirit to the witness stand and the Holy Spirit testifies that you have eternal life. All three testified to the fact that you have eternal life.

These three, I believe, are the three baptisms available to each person: "the blood" is the blood of Jesus sprinkled on our heart when we were baptized into Christ (justification)[K] ; "the water" is water baptism; "the Spirit" is the baptism of the Holy Spirit. But to complete the picture, we need to modify our image of the courtroom in this way: as each witness comes forward, the "judge" changes. For the blood, the judge is the Father; the blood testifies to the Father that a person has eternal life: "When I see the blood I will pass over" (Exodus 12:13); only the Father sees the blood. For the water, the judge is the world; the water testifies to the world that someone has eternal life; it's the world that sees a person's water baptism. And lastly for the Spirit, the judge is you, yourself.; the Holy Spirit testifies to the born-again person within his own heart that he has eternal life: "the Spirit Himself bears witness with our spirit that we are children of God" (Romans 8:16). One of the by-products of the baptism of the Holy Spirit is a new assurance within a person that they truly are born again. They already were before they received the baptism of the Spirit, but after receiving the baptism of the Spirit they have a new confidence about it.

So, what is water baptism? It's a way to respond to the preaching of the gospel, a burial service for the old nature, a new separation from the attractions of the world-system, and a witness that this person has eternal life.

Endnotes, Chapter 8

G The King James Version translators sometimes translated *baptizo* as "dip" -- for instance when Jesus dipped the bread in the sauce and gave it to Judas (John 13:26) -- but more often transliterated it into "baptize," possibly because of pressure to be politically correct. See Luke 16:24 & Revelation 19:13 for other times *baptizo* is translated "dip."

H When the word "baptized" stands by itself without specifying "into _____," it is talking about water baptism. But sometimes it specifies something else as the medium into which the person is being baptized, for instance "baptized in the Holy Spirit" or "baptized into Christ."

I *"Now these things happened to them as an example, and they were written for our instruction" (1 Corinthians 10:11).*

J As this typology of the Christian life continues, after a time in the wilderness they crossed another body of water, the Jordan River, into the Promised Land. In old hymns you'll find the Jordan being used as a picture of death and the Promised Land as Heaven, but that doesn't fit the Israelites' history, for Canaan had not only grapes but giants! In fact, the Israelites had more battles in Canaan than before crossing Jordan, but there will be no battles in heaven, so Canaan can't be heaven. The Promised Land is a picture of the Spirit-filled life, and Jordan pictures the baptism of the Holy Spirit.

K *Hebrews 10:19 "Since therefore, brethren, we have confidence to enter the holy place by the blood of Jesus...(verse 22) let us draw near with a sincere heart in full assurance of faith, having our hearts sprinkled clean from an evil conscience." Hebrews 12:22 "But you have come...(verse 24) to Jesus, the mediator of a new covenant, and to the sprinkled blood, which speaks better than the blood of Abel."*

Chapter Nine
The Baptism of the Holy Spirit

Who is the Holy Spirit?

> *John 14:16 And I will ask the Father, and He will give you another Helper, that He may be with you forever.*

Jesus describes the Holy Spirit as "another Helper," *allos Paracletos* in Greek. The Greek word *allos* means "another of the same kind." Jesus' use of *allos* highlights that the Holy Spirit would be the same kind of helper as He Himself had been to the disciples. "Helper" always sounded to me like a secondary role, as we would use it in talking about a carpenter's helper – the carpenter does most of the work while the helper fetches tools and materials. But then I learned that when a small ship was having trouble coming into the harbor, the Greeks would send a big ship to come alongside it to help it get in safely. The big ship was called the *Paracletos*. This changed my image of the Helper available to us! We are the small ship having trouble, and the Holy Spirit is our big, powerful Helper who can come alongside us.

> *John 16:7 But I tell you the truth, it is to your advantage that I go away; for if I do not go away, the Helper shall not come to you; but if I go, I will send Him to you.*

> *John 16:13-14 But when He, the Spirit of truth, comes, He will guide you into all the truth; for He will not speak on His own initiative, but whatever He hears, He will speak; and He will disclose to you what is to come. He shall glorify Me; for He shall take of Mine, and shall disclose it to you.*

The Holy Spirit is a person and He is God, the third person of the Trinity. Part of His ministry is to show us more about Jesus by taking things that belong to Jesus and making them real to us. One picture of the Holy Spirit in the Old Testament was the dew that brought the manna. The bread of life came via the dew, then the dew evaporated so that all you saw was the manna. That's how the Holy Spirit is; He wants to present more about Jesus to us and then withdraw to the background.

"Baptized"?! with the Holy Spirit?

When we see the word "baptize," we automatically think of water, and it takes some rethinking for us to realize that there are other baptisms besides water baptism. For years Christians read the verses that we're about to read and ignored them, thinking that it was something to do with water baptism. But notice that the baptism of the Spirit is <u>contrasted</u> with water baptism in the next verses.

> Luke 3:16 John answered and said to them all, "As for me, I baptize you with water; but One is coming who is mightier than I, and I am not fit to untie the thong of His sandals; He Himself will baptize you with the Holy Spirit and fire."
>
> Acts 1:5 for John baptized with water, but you shall be baptized with the Holy Spirit.

Jesus Himself is the officiant at this baptism, the one who performs it. And the medium (what we are baptized with) is not water but the Holy Spirit Himself.

Why Do I Need this Baptism of the Holy Spirit?

> Acts 1:4-9 And gathering them together, He commanded them not to leave Jerusalem, but to wait for what the Father had promised. "Which," He said, "you heard of from Me; for John baptized with water, but you shall be

> *baptized with the Holy Spirit not many days from now."
> And so when they had come together, they were asking
> Him, saying, "Lord, is it at this time You are restoring
> the kingdom to Israel?" He said to them, "It is not for
> you to know times or epochs which the Father has fixed
> by His own authority; but you shall receive power when
> the Holy Spirit has come upon you; and you shall be My
> witnesses both in Jerusalem, and in all Judea and
> Samaria, and even to the remotest part of the earth."*

Jesus' last words before His ascension must hold special significance for us! We see that the disciples had no idea what to expect, and thought that the experience Jesus was predicting might have to do with receiving political power over the Romans. Jesus said they would receive power through this baptism, but not political power. Instead, the power would be power to be His witnesses. I want to put the emphasis on "to be" a witness. The power of the Holy Spirit is first of all power that transforms our lives into lives that are a witness for Christ, not just a power to help us have better words for telling people the good news.

Some Christians say that they don't feel a need for more power in their lives. If this is true of you, I suspect that you may have already been baptized in the Holy Spirit without knowing it, or that this is not what God is doing with you at this time. But if you ever get to a place where you long for a real change in your life, I'd recommend starting here.

The King James Version translates two Greek words as "power": *exousia* and *dunamis*. *Exousia* emphasizes the authority - the right - to do something (as in John 1:12) while *dunamis* emphasizes the ability to do it - the might. One is like the policeman's badge while the other is his physical strength and handcuffs, etc. In this passage the word is *dunamis*. They would receive the ability to be witnesses for Him. And we have to conclude as we read the subsequent history that these 120 people did receive something that began to transform the world, something that changed them from people who were hiding from the authorities into bold witnesses of the resurrection.

Here's another comparison that may help us understand the difference between being a Christian without the baptism of the Holy Spirit and being a Christian who has received the baptism of the Spirit. I'm sorry if it offends some; it's not my comparison but Jesus'. In John 4, Jesus told the woman at the well that salvation would be like a well or spring of water: John 4:14 "...the water that I shall give him shall become in him a well of water springing up to eternal life." But in John 7, the scripture compares the Spirit to rivers of water. John 7:38-39 "'He who believes in Me, as the Scripture said, "From his innermost being shall flow rivers of living water."' But this He spoke of the Spirit, whom those who believed in Him were to receive; for the Spirit was not yet given, because Jesus was not yet glorified." If you want to deliver water to a town, you can dig wells or divert rivers. It's all water, but a quantitative difference in results.

What Happened on the Day of Pentecost

Acts 2:1-13, 37-39 And when the day of Pentecost had come, they were all together in one place. And suddenly there came from heaven a noise like a violent, rushing wind, and it filled the whole house where they were sitting. And there appeared to them tongues as of fire distributing themselves, and they rested on each one of them. And they were all filled with the Holy Spirit and began to speak with other tongues, as the Spirit was giving them utterance. Now there were Jews living in Jerusalem, devout men, from every nation under heaven. And when this sound occurred, the multitude came together, and were bewildered, because they were each one hearing them speak in his own language. And they were amazed and marveled, saying, "Why, are not all these who are speaking Galileans? And how is it that we

> *each hear them in our own language to which we were born? Parthinans and Medes and Elamites, and residents of Mesopotamia, Judea and Cappadocia, Pontus and Asia, Phrygia and Pamphylia, Egypt and the districts of Libya around Cyrene, and visitors from Rome, both Jews and proselytes, Cretans and Arabs – we hear them in our own tongues speaking of the mighty deeds of God." And they all continued in amazement and great perplexity, saying to one another, "What does this mean?" But others were mocking and saying, "They are full of sweet wine." ...*
>
> *(Verse 37) Now when they heard this [Peter's preaching], they were pierced to the heart, and said to Peter and the rest of the apostles, "Brethren, what shall we do?" And Peter said to them, "Repent, and let each of you be baptized in the name of Jesus Christ [in water] for the forgiveness of your sins; and you shall receive the gift of the Holy Spirit. For the promise is for you and for your children, and for all who are far off, as many as the Lord our God shall call to Himself."*

All this happened in the same city where Jesus was killed less than two months before! A loud noise as if from a violent wind rushed across the sky and filled the house.[L] This noise drew a crowd who came to see what happened. Inside the house, flames that looked like fire distributed themselves on each person, they were filled with the Holy Spirit, and received the supernatural ability to speak in languages they had never learned. The fact that these were actual languages and not gibberish was confirmed as they poured out in the street, and the people from many foreign nations and languages heard them telling about the mighty deeds of God. The crowd became ecstatic and were eager to hear what this was all about. Sometimes you'll hear the gift of tongues referred to as an "ecstatic utterance," but it is the onlookers who are described as "ecstatic" in verses 7 and 12, not the 120 who were speaking in tongues. The gift of tongues is not dependent on a person's emotions.

Questions about the Baptism of the Holy Spirit

- **Didn't I receive everything when I got saved?**

Acts 8:5-6, 12, 14-17 And Philip went down to the city of Samaria and began proclaiming Christ to them. And the multitudes with one accord were giving attention to what was said by Philip, as they heard and saw the signs which he was performing. ... (verse 12) But when they believed Philip preaching the good news about the kingdom of God and the name of Jesus Christ, they were being baptized, men and women alike. ... (verse 14) Now when the apostles in Jerusalem heard that Samaria had received the word of God, they sent them Peter and John, who came down and prayed for them, that they might receive the Holy Spirit. For He had not yet fallen upon any of them; they had simply been baptized in the name of the Lord Jesus. Then they began laying their hands on them, and they were receiving the Holy Spirit.

We have to conclude by the narrative of verse 12 that the Samaritans were saved, because it records that they both believed the good news and were being baptized in water. But verse 15 says that had not yet received the Holy Spirit. And to make it doubly clear, they only received the Holy Spirit after Peter and John could come from Jerusalem and lay hands on them.

- **Why do some say that the supernatural gifts have ceased?**

This is usually based on misinterpreting the last part of 1 Corinthians 13.

> *1 Corinthians 13:8-13 Love never fails; but if there are gifts of prophecy, they will be done away; if there are tongues, they will cease; if there is knowledge, it will be done away. For we know in part, and we prophesy in part; but when the perfect comes, the partial will be done away. When I was a child, I used to speak as a child, think as a child, reason as a child; when I became a man, I did away with childish things. For now we see in a mirror dimly, but then face to face; now I know in part, but then I shall know fully just as I also have been fully known. But now abide faith, hope, love, these three; but the greatest of these is love.*

Supernatural gifts <u>will</u> cease one day, but what does the passage say about when? "When the perfect comes" (v.10). The question is, when is that? The teaching that the gifts have ceased holds that "the perfect" is the Bible and concludes that supernatural gifts like tongues and prophesy ceased when the compiling of the Bible was complete. But notice what else happens when the perfect comes:

verse 8 - knowledge will cease (Gr. *gnosis,* - partial knowledge by experience, by reasoning, science);

verse 12 - we will see face to face; and

verse 12 - we will know fully (Gr. *epignosis*). "The perfect" is when we see Jesus, when all our partial knowledge is swept into a full revelation of Him! The teaching that the gifts ceased ignores the fact that when tongues and prophecy cease, science and all our partial knowledge also ceases.

- **What role does speaking in tongues have in the baptism of the Spirit?**

Five times in Acts people received the initial filling of the Holy Spirit. Let's examine what visible manifestations there were each time:

Acts 2:1-4 And when the day of Pentecost had come, they were all together in one place. And suddenly there came from heaven a noise like a violent, rushing wind, and it filled the whole house where they were sitting. And there appeared to them tongues as of fire distributing themselves, and they rested on each one of them. And they were all filled with the Holy Spirit and began to speak with other tongues, as the Spirit was giving them utterance.

Acts 8:14-19 Now when the apostles in Jerusalem heard that Samaria had received the word of God, they sent them Peter and John, who came down and prayed for them, that they might receive the Holy Spirit. For He had not yet fallen upon any of them; they had simply been baptized in the name of the Lord Jesus. Then they began laying their hands on them, and they were receiving the Holy Spirit. Now when Simon saw that the Spirit was bestowed through the laying on of the apostles' hands, he offered them money, saying, "Give this authority to me as well, so that everyone on whom I lay my hands may receive the Holy Spirit."

Acts 9:17-19 And Ananias departed and entered the house, and after laying his hands on him said, "Brother Saul, the Lord Jesus, who appeared to you on the road by which you were coming, has sent me so that you may regain your sight, and be filled with the Holy Spirit." And immediately there fell from his eyes something like scales, and he regained his sight, and he arose and was baptized; and he took food and was strengthened.

Acts 10:44-46 While Peter was still speaking these words, the Holy Spirit fell upon all those who were listening to the message. And all the circumcised believers who had come with Peter were amazed, because the gift of the Holy Spirit had been poured out upon the Gentiles also.

For they were hearing them speaking with tongues and exalting God.

Acts 19:6 And when Paul had laid his hands upon them, the Holy Spirit came on them, and they began speaking with tongues and prophesying.

Reference	What happened....
Acts 2:1-4	Noise of strong wind, flames of fire, speaking in tongues
Acts 8:14-19	Something spectacular because of Simon's reaction, but unspecified
Acts 9:17-19	Nothing noted. At some point Paul did receive the gift of tongues (1 Cor. 14:18), either at this time or later.
Acts 10:44-46	Speaking in tongues, by which the Jewish believers recognized that the Gentiles had received the Holy Spirit
Acts 19:6	Speaking in tongues, prophesying

Three out of five times includes speaking in tongues, which is the only manifestation that repeats. But in two of the occurrences, there is a loud silence about anything specific that happened. To me, this is a clue that we need to be careful about being dogmatic that any one specific thing must happen when a person receives the baptism of the Holy Spirit. Many things happen to people when they receive the Spirit, and the most common is that they receive the gift of speaking in tongues. But I can't be dogmatic and say "You must speak in tongues to have been baptized in the Holy Spirit," because the Bible never says that. My hunch is that some people have been baptized in the Spirit who have never spoken in tongues. At the same time, I look for the normal evidence to be that a person will receive this gift when they are baptized with the Spirit.

In my own experience, I suspect that I was filled with the Spirit six months before I ever spoke in other tongues. I had a dramatic experience with the Lord in which I had a vision and was filled up with joy, and after that my life really changed. The most dramatic change was that the Bible came alive to me where before this experience I read it from a sense of duty. I had been a Christian for four years, but much more joy and enthusiasm came into my relationship with the Lord Jesus. Suddenly God's word was speaking right to me, and it was wonderful. After this experience I had a desire to speak in tongues but I didn't understand that God doesn't violate our will, He doesn't just move our mouths without our cooperation. So I would pray and wait for God to start manipulating my mouth, but nothing happened. After six months of struggling with this, a traveling evangelist came through town who understood more perfectly. He explained that Acts 2 says "they spoke" as the Spirit "gave them the ability," and that in faith we had to begin to speak, but not in a language we know, believing God to give the ability. When he prayed for me I stepped out in faith and started to speak -- I didn't know what would come out -- and my tongue began speaking a foreign language. So, I can't be sure I was filled with the Spirit before receiving the gift of tongues, but I strongly suspect that I was. There are probably a lot of Christians in the same situation, who because of misunderstanding or wrong teaching have not received a manifestation of any supernatural gift, but who have received the baptism of the Holy Spirit at one time.

• Can anything block a believer from receiving?

I hesitate to even mention this area because I don't want to discourage anyone who is seeking, but there are a couple things that can block a believer from receiving. After I was first baptized in the Spirit I attended a youth meeting every Saturday night. At the end of the meetings the host always invited anyone who wanted the baptism of the

Spirit to go to a separate room, along with anyone who wanted to pray with them. So I always went there and got a lot of practice praying for people to receive the baptism of the Holy Spirit. Out of that experience I learned some practical tips.

Two things that the Bible says block our prayers are unconfessed sin and unforgiveness:

Psalm 66:18 If I regard wickedness in my heart; The Lord will not hear.

Mark 11:25 And whenever you stand praying, forgive, if you have anything against anyone; so that your Father also who is in heaven may forgive you your transgressions.

So if something comes to mind as you read those scriptures you'll want to get with the Lord Jesus about it.

But the more common area that I've seen prevent people from receiving is involvement in the occult. Somehow, dabbling with these things, even "innocently," puts up a roadblock to the move of the Spirit.

Deuteronomy 18:10-12 There shall not be found among you anyone who makes his son or his daughter pass through the fire, one who uses divination [fortune-telling, tarot cards, palm reading, etc.], *one who practices witchcraft, or one who interprets omens* [astrology, horoscopes, tea-leaf reading, crystal ball, eight-ball], *or a sorcerer, or one who casts a spell, or a medium, or a spiritist* [séances, Ouija board, automatic writing], *or one who calls up the dead. For whoever does these things is detestable to the LORD.*

Involvement with these things, even innocent "play" with them as a child, can sometimes block a person from receiving. Many times we would be praying for someone and nothing would be happening. So we would stop and ask if he or she had any occult involvement in the past. "Oh, no, not at all!" was usually the response. Then we would ask if they ever tried to levitate someone at a slumber party or read the horoscope. "Oh sure, but I didn't mean anything by it!" Well, they may not have taken it seriously, but the evil powers did!

These blockages are easily unstopped, because of the power available to us. If you've had any involvement (even reading a horoscope out of curiosity), do these two things: 1) ask the Lord to forgive you; and 2) renounce each thing by name, i.e. pray with someone and say, "I renounce reading the horoscope in Jesus' name; I renounce playing with the Ouija board in Jesus' name, etc." To renounce it means you are putting it behind you and never want anything to do with it again. Doing this removes the blockage, and normally the person would easily receive the baptism of the Spirit afterward.

• What are the qualifications to receive the baptism of the Holy Spirit?

There are only two: 1) You must be saved. John 14:17 "the Spirit of Truth, whom the world cannot receive..." and 2) You must ask! Luke 11:13 "If you then, being evil, know how to give good gifts to your children, how much more shall your Heavenly Father give the Holy Spirit to those who ask Him?"

A common mistake is to feel like we have to get "good enough" or holy enough to be worthy to pray for the Holy Spirit. But we don't get good to get the Spirit, in fact we need the Spirit's power to help us! Paul addresses this in Galatians 3:1-2 "You foolish Galatians...This is the only thing I want to find out from you: Did you receive the Spirit by the works of law, or by the hearing with faith?" Receiving is not by works, it is purely a gift!

If you haven't asked before now, this is a good time! Remember that your Savior, Jesus, is the Baptizer. Spend some time worshipping Him, and then ask! Or better yet, if you know someone who is already baptized in the Spirit who would be willing to pray with you, get together and ask together.

Endnotes, Chapter 9

^L Jesus compared the Spirit to a wind in *John 3:8 "The wind blows where it wishes and you hear the sound of it, but do not know where it comes from and where it is going; so is everyone who is born of the Spirit."* Also, the Hebrew word for "breath" and "spirit" is the same.

Chapter Ten
Resurrections of the Dead

If we step back for a minute to look at the big picture of where we've been in our study together, it would be fair to say that everything that we have studied so far has been connected with salvation -- either with justification, or sanctification, or both. Even the chapters about baptisms fit in to our study of sanctification, for we learned that water baptism is part of sanctification in that it separates the believer from the pull of the world, and the baptism of the Holy Spirit gives a believer new power to be a witness.

In the next chapters we will investigate the third part of salvation --the future salvation of the body-- and the eternal judgments that both believers and unbelievers will face. Our culture has much false information, wishful thinking, and even psychological denial concerning the afterlife. Hopefully our study will liberate us from false ideas we've unknowingly bought into and help us understand what the Bible teaches about the life to come.

Will the Dead Be Raised?

We begin by asking what will happen to the bodies of those who have died. Will the bodies of the dead really rise again? Most people seem to suspect that the soul of a deceased person continues to exist into the afterlife, but what about the body? Does the physical matter of a person's body have any significance for eternity?

> *John 6:37-40 All that the Father gives Me shall come to Me, and the one who comes to Me I will certainly not cast out. For I have come down from heaven, not to do My*

> *own will, but the will of Him who sent Me. And this is the will of Him who sent Me, that of all that He has given Me I lose nothing, but raise it up on the last day. For this is the will of My Father, that everyone who beholds the Son and believes in Him, may have eternal life; and I Myself will raise him up on the last day.*

Jesus declares that He will resurrect all those who have believed in Him. Everyone who has eternal life will be raised from the dead "on the last day."

Will only Believers Be Raised?

In the next reference, we learn that Jesus also promised a resurrection for non-believers. Thus there will be two resurrections: a resurrection of believers to eternal life and a resurrection of unbelievers to judgment. John 5:28-29 "For an hour is coming in which all who are in the tombs shall hear His voice, and shall come forth; those who did the good to a resurrection of life, those who committed the evil to a resurrection of judgment." Paul echoes this thought in his defense to Governor Felix in Acts 24:15, "There shall certainly be a resurrection of both the righteous and the wicked." Believers and non-believers will experience a resurrection. Think about the details of this! It means that each person's physical body will be brought back together from wherever it decomposed, reunited with the soul and brought to life. The branch of physics called thermodynamics teaches us that matter can change its form but cannot be destroyed, and I have to conclude that God keeps track of every atom: the very atoms that make up a person's body will furnish the "raw material" which will be transformed into imperishable bodies. I heard of a man who did not want to be found by God on resurrection day and therefore directed in his will that he be cremated and his ashes scattered across the Atlantic. Will this hide him from God? Not at all; God keeps track of everything. If forensic science can gather shed skin cells from a doorknob or hairbrush and recapture the person's DNA, how much does God need?

> *1 Corinthians 15:12-20 Now if Christ is preached, that He has been raised from the dead, how do some among you say that there is no resurrection of the dead? But if there is no resurrection of the dead, not even Christ has been raised; and if Christ has not been raised, then our preaching is vain, your faith also is vain. Moreover we are even found to be false witnesses of God, because we witnessed against God that He raised Christ, whom He did not raise, if in fact the dead are not raised. For if the dead are not raised, not even Christ has been raised; and if Christ has not been raised, your faith is worthless; you are still in your sins. Then those also who have fallen asleep in Christ have perished. If we have hoped in Christ in this life only, we are of all men most to be pitied. But now Christ has been raised from the dead, the first fruits of those who are asleep.*

The apostle is very bold here, and declares that our Christian faith stands or falls on this historical event: either Christ was raised from the dead or He was not. If He was not, then our faith is useless and we are still guilty because of our sins. But He was raised, and it changes everything. This fact is the central truth of Christianity.

Death is a great enemy of mankind. Death was not in God's original plan for men, but ever since it made its entrance into history it has been 100% effective. Think of all the soldiers that have died in wars, all the cancer victims, and all the heart attack deaths. Think of the fear that death has provoked, and how many have lived without comfort because of a constant dread of death. Death is called the "last enemy" (1 Corinthians 15:26). Now at last we have someone who has experienced death (not just a "near-death experience," but the real thing, being dead for three days), who has come back from the other side of the grave, never to die again, proving that death can be defeated!

Jesus' resurrection proves to us that death is not the end, and holds the promise that death itself will one day be vanquished and its effects erased, when we receive our bodies back again.

When Are The Dead Raised?

> *Daniel 12:1-2 Now at that time Michael, the great prince who stands guard over the sons of your people, will arise. And there will be a time of distress such as never occurred since there was a nation until that time; and at that time your people, everyone who is found written in the book, will be rescued. And many of those who sleep in the dust of the ground will awake, these to everlasting life, but the others to disgrace and everlasting contempt.*

This is one of the most famous passages in the Old Testament about the resurrection from the dead. Daniel prophesied of "a time of distress, then many [not all] of those who sleep in the dust will awake, these [who awake at that time] to everlasting life, but the others [who do not awake at that time] to everlasting contempt." From Daniel we learn that the resurrections do not happen at the same time: the resurrection of those that Daniel says are "written in the book" will be separate from the second resurrection that we read about in John chapter 5. First comes a resurrection of life, and later a resurrection of judgment.

Our next scripture has more detail about the two resurrections.

> *1 Corinthians 15:22-24 For as in Adam all die, so also in Christ all shall be made alive [the Greek does not mean "made alive" in the sense of eternal life, but "raised up"]. But each in his own order: 1) Christ the first fruits, 2) after that those who are Christ's at His coming, 3) then comes the end, when He delivers up the kingdom to the God and Father, when He has abolished all rule and all authority and power.*

The order of the resurrections is laid out clearly:

Christ was first to be raised from the dead. Jesus' resurrection is seen as part of the first resurrection, the "first fruits" of it. The analogy is of a harvest where the first fruits of the crop are brought in, and then the same harvest continues with more of the same crop.

After that, those who belong to Him will be raised when He comes again.

"Then comes the end" when the rest of the dead will be raised.

So the first resurrection began when Jesus was raised and concludes when He comes again and believers in Him are raised from the dead. Then the second resurrection comes at "the end," sometime later than the return of Christ.

> *Revelation 20:4-5, 7, 11-15 And I saw thrones, and they sat upon them, and judgment was given to them. And I saw the souls of those who had been beheaded because of the testimony of Jesus and because of the word of God, and those who had not worshiped the beast or his image, and had not received the mark upon their forehead and upon their hand; and they came to life and reigned with Christ for a thousand years. The rest of the dead did not come to life until the thousand years were completed. This is the first resurrection. ... (verse 7) And when the thousand years are completed, ... (verse 11) I saw a great white throne and Him who sat upon it, from whose presence earth and heaven fled away, and no place was found for them. And I saw the dead, the great and the small, standing before the throne, and books were opened; and another book was opened, which is the book of life; and the dead were judged from the things which were written in the books, according to their deeds. And the sea gave up the dead which were in it, and death and Hades gave up the dead which were in them; and they were judged, every one of them according to their deeds. And death and Hades were*

> *thrown into the lake of fire. This is the second death, the lake of fire. And if anyone's name was not found written in the book of life, he was thrown into the lake of fire.*

This scripture speaks of the "first resurrection," then the millennium (from Latin mille, thousand; annum, year), then the rest of the dead being raised to stand for judgment before the "great white throne." Here the gap of time between the resurrections is described as lasting a definite length of time, namely one thousand years. (For a brief explanation of three different interpretations of the millennium, see Appendix B.)

Where is a Believer between Death and Resurrection?

What happens to the consciousness of a Christian between death and resurrection? Some teach that the soul sleeps along with the body while others teach that the soul goes immediately to be with God. Which is correct?

> *2 Corinthians 5:8 We are of good courage, I say, and prefer rather to be absent from the body and to be at home with the Lord.*

Paul equates "absent from the body" with "at home with the Lord." So our souls will not be asleep, but with God. This is confirmed by a careful reading of our next scripture.

> *1 Thessalonians 4:13-18 But we do not want you to be uninformed, brethren, about those who are asleep [Christians who have died], that you may not grieve, as do the rest who have no hope. For if we believe that Jesus died and rose again, even so God will bring with Him those who have fallen asleep in Jesus. For this we say to you by the word of the Lord, that we who are alive, and remain until the coming of the Lord, shall not precede those who have fallen asleep. For the Lord Himself will descend from heaven with a shout, with the voice of the archangel, and with the trumpet of God; and*

> *the dead in Christ shall rise first. Then we who are alive
> and remain shall be caught up together with them in
> the clouds to meet the Lord in the air, and thus we shall
> always be with the Lord. Therefore comfort one
> another with these words.*

Verse 14 talks about God bringing "with Him those who have fallen asleep in Jesus," that is, the souls of all believers. Then verse 16 says, "and the dead in Christ will rise first," meaning the bodies. The soul, which has been with God, will return as the Lord's shout goes forth and raises the body from the dead, then soul and body will be reunited there in the air. This event, the catching up of living believers and reuniting of the souls and bodies of believers who have already died, is popularly called "the rapture" (a term is not found in scripture).

What Kind of Body will Believers Have?

> *Philippians 3:20-21 We eagerly wait for a Savior, the Lord
> Jesus Christ, who will transform the body of our
> humiliation into conformity with the body of His glory.*

> *1 Corinthians 15:35-38, 42-44 But someone will say, "How
> are the dead raised? And with what kind of body do
> they come? You fool! That which you sow does not
> come to life unless it dies; and that which you sow, you
> do not sow the body which is to be, but a bare grain,
> perhaps of wheat or of something else. But God gives it
> a body just as He wished, and to each of the seeds a body
> of its own. ... (verse 42) So also is the resurrection of the
> dead. It is sown a perishable body, it is raised an
> imperishable body; it is sown in dishonor, it is raised in
> glory; it is sown in weakness, it is raised in power; it is
> sown a natural body, it is raised a spiritual body. If
> there is a natural body, there is also a spiritual body.*

(Psst, I have to let you in on this, that every time the Bible poses a question and then says, "You fool!", I've usually had that question!)

Paul compares the transformation that will change the physical body into a spiritual body with the trans-formation of a single grain of corn into a stalk of corn. One grain of corn is sown, and a stalk of corn grows from it; thus the two are related but different. The corn stalk and ear looks quite different than the corn grain. In a similar way our new bodies will be related to our present bodies, but different. Our present bodies are described as perishable, dishonorable, weak, and natural. Our next bodies will be imperishable, glorious, powerful, and spiritual. What was perishable will become imperishable; what was dishonorable will become glorious; what was weak will become powerful; and what was natural (the literal Greek is "soulish") will become spiritual.

Present Bodies	Future Bodies
Perishable	Imperishable
Dishonorable	Glorious
Weak	Powerful
Natural *(Soulish)*	Spiritual

This physical body we have is not made for heaven but for earth. Do you remember the story of Moses' request to see God's glory and God's reply? "But He said, 'You cannot see My face, for no man can see Me and live!'" (Exodus 33:20). Apparently, it's a physical impossibility; you cannot see God face to face in the body you have. We cannot even stare directly at the glory of the sun without damaging our eyesight -- how much less could we look at the full glory of God! So we need a different kind of body that is fitted for the intensity of glory that we will experience in the next life.

But I find myself asking how something can be a "spiritual" "body"?" I think of "spiritual" as meaning without substance or matter, whereas "body" means it has substance; the two don't seem to go together. The Greek helps here. In the last pair of contrasts in verse 44, the contrast to "spiritual" in literal Greek is "soulish," which means that the contrast Paul is drawing is not between a material body and an immaterial body, but between a <u>soulish</u> body and a <u>spiritual</u> body.

> 1 Corinthians 15:44 refers to a body *psuchikon*, an animalistic or physical body governed by the soul or animal or fallen instinct of man, and a body *pneumatikon*, spiritual, governed by the divine quality in man, the spirit. (Spiros Zodhiates, Th.D, *The Complete Word Study New Testament*, AMG Publishers, 1991, p.956.)

We can describe physical objects two different ways: by the material from which they are made, or the use to which they are put. For instance, two cups can be described by what they are made of or by the liquids they carry. A cup can be described as a china or plastic cup if we are thinking about its material or as a coffee cup or juice cup if referring to its use. When Paul describes our new bodies as "spiritual" bodies, he is not describing the material from which they will be made, but their use, what they will be designed to express or contain. Both old and new bodies are substantive – you can feel and touch them, so they are material and "real" -- but the difference is that our present bodies are made to express our souls, while our resurrected bodies will be made to express our spirits. (Credit for this explanation goes to N.T. Wright, from a lecture.)

The passage from 1 Corinthians 15 goes on to contrast Jesus and Adam, and says "just as we have borne the image of the earthy, we shall bear the image of the heavenly" (v.49). So if we want to know what our new bodies will be like and what capabilities they will have, we can think of Jesus' body. It was physical, it could be touched, it ate a fish, but it could also appear and disappear and walk through walls. (See Luke 24:36-43.) Our new bodies will be like Jesus' resurrected body.

Let's conclude with Paul's triumphant words from the end of chapter 15 of 1 Corinthians.

> *1 Corinthians 15:51-54 Behold, I tell you a mystery: we shall not all sleep, but we shall all be changed, in a moment, in the twinkling of an eye, at the last trumpet; for the trumpet will sound, and the dead will be raised imperishable, and we shall be changed. For this perishable must put on the imperishable, and this mortal must put on immortality. But when this perishable will have put on the imperishable, and this mortal will have put on immortality, then will come about the saying that is written, "Death is swallowed up in victory."*

Chapter Eleven
The Believers' Judgment of Rewards

John 5:24 is one of Jesus' "truly, truly" statements. The double emphasis at the beginning [literally, "amen, amen"] alerts us that something especially significant is coming.

> *John 5:24 Truly, truly, I say to you, he who hears My word, and believes Him who sent Me, has eternal life,* [Pause right there. The believer, Jesus says, has eternal life -- present tense -- already. So when does eternal life begin? Not after we die, but the moment we believe in Jesus our eternal life has begun.] *and does not come into judgment, but has passed out of death into life.*

Believers will not be judged in the future; they have escaped the wrath of God. Other scriptures restate this same truth: John 3:18 "He who believes in Him is not judged." Romans 8:1 "There is therefore now no condemnation for those who are in Christ Jesus." There is nothing to condemn those who are "in Christ!" The judgment that believers will <u>not</u> face is the judgment about whether they have eternal life or not.

But, since this is so, we are puzzled by scriptures that do speak of believers facing a judgment, such as

> *2 Corinthians 5:10 For we must all appear before the judgment seat of Christ, that each one may be recompensed for his deeds in the body, according to what he has done, whether good or bad.*

How do we reconcile this with John 5:24?

Notice 2 Corinthians 5 talks about <u>recompense</u> (reward) for deeds. When we studied justification, we learned that no person will be justified by his deeds (Titus 3:5, Romans 3:20, etc.). So, a judgment of deeds of believers is not to determine their going to heaven; that was already decided when they put their faith in Jesus' finished work. But there is more to heaven than just going there! There is also reward in heaven, as Jesus talked about in Matthew 6:1 "Beware of practicing your righteousness before men to be noticed by them; otherwise you will have no reward with your Father who is in heaven." In this passage from the Sermon on the Mount, Jesus was talking about "reward in heaven." 2 Corinthians 5 shows us Christ on a judgment seat with believers appearing before Him, to be recompensed for good deeds or bad deeds, i.e. to be rewarded for their sanctification or to lose reward because of a lack of sanctification. Eternal life is not based on deeds but on grace and faith. Eternal reward is based on deeds. The deeds we have done as believers will determine our reward after we are in heaven.

The next scripture goes into some detail about this judgment of deeds. Paul makes the analogy that the Christian life is like constructing a building.

> *1 Corinthians 3:9-15 For we are God's fellow workers; you are God's field, God's building. According to the grace of God which was given to me, as a wise master builder I laid a foundation, and another is building upon it. But let each man be careful how he builds upon it. For no man can lay a foundation other than the one which is laid, which is Jesus Christ. Now if any man builds upon the foundation with gold, silver, precious stones, wood, hay, straw, each man's work will become evident; for the day will show it, because it is to be revealed with fire; and the fire itself will test the quality of each man's work. If any man's work which he has built upon it*

remains, he shall receive a reward. If any man's work is burned up, he shall suffer loss; but he himself shall be saved, yet so as through fire.

The foundation of the building (v.11) is Jesus Christ in the person's life. Then upon the foundation each person is building with some type of material. Each good thing we do is like adding one more bit of gold, silver, or a precious gem to the structure. Each bad or

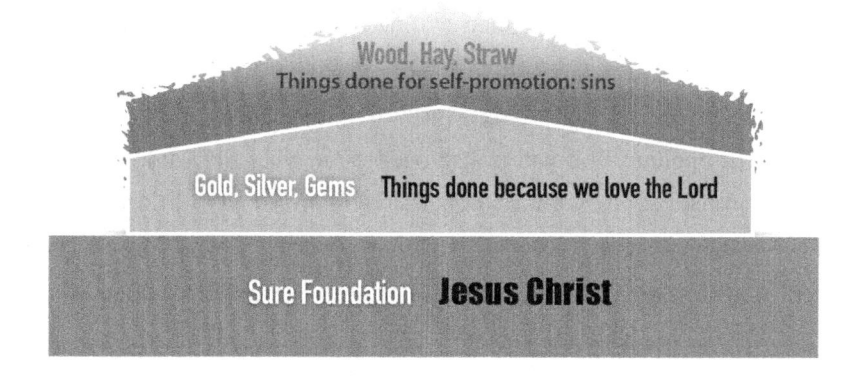

Wood, Hay, Straw — Things done for self-promotion: sins

Gold, Silver, Gems Things done because we love the Lord

Sure Foundation **Jesus Christ**

selfish thing is adding wood, hay, or straw. Since wood does not burn up as quickly as straw, we conclude that some bad deeds are not as bad as others, but in the end both burn. The main difference is that gold, silver, and gemstones can withstand a fire while wood, hay, and straw cannot.

We can draw some conclusions from this passage:

When a building burns down, the foundation remains. The foundation of Jesus in a person's life (if indeed they have been born again) remains after the fire. We conclude from this and from verse 15 that it is possible for a person to have <u>no</u> reward, yet be saved. "Saved, yet so as through fire," v.15 says -- like someone who escaped from a burning house with his life but nothing else. So it must be possible for a Christian to lose all reward but still have Jesus as his foundation and go to heaven.

The fire tests "the quality of each man's work." We tend to be impressed by quantity, but the testing of that day will be examining the quality of our works.

"The day will show it." Some things we are impressed with now will be very unimpressive when "the day" shows them. All facades will be stripped away and the motives of men's hearts will be revealed (1 Corinthians 4:5) so that we will see not only <u>what</u> a person did but <u>why</u> he did it, and the secrets of men will be revealed. The reverse is also true: some unimpressive things will be seen in their true light and will be impressive. Some things forgotten and unrewarded will be rewarded openly. God will praise people for what they did! We are always praising God, but in that day God will praise men: 1 Corinthians 4:5, "each man's praise will come to him from God." But "before we can hear God say, 'Well done!' we have to do well!" (a quote from a talk by Costa Deir of Elim Bible Institute).

A famous preacher shared a dream he had about receiving his reward from the Lord. In his dream, he was walking down a long aisle toward God's throne to receive his reward. In God's hand was a beautiful crown. To the preacher's annoyance he noticed the cleaning lady from the church walking beside him, and soon noticed that along with the crown in Jesus' hands, He also had a paper hat. The preacher thought to himself, "How sad that the paper hat is all the reward this lady will get." Then Jesus placed the crown on her and the paper hat on him! The lesson he took away from this dream was that the success of his ministry was not due to his preaching but to her prayers.

> *Romans 14:10b, 12 "For we shall all stand before the judgment seat of God. ... So then each one of us shall give account of himself to God."*

We will give an account of ourselves -- not our parents or other people, but we ourselves -- what we did with our responsibilities and gifts, and what we neglected to do.

Lessons about Rewards from the Parable of the Talents[M]

> *Matthew 25:14-30 For it is just like a man about to go on a journey, who called his own slaves, and entrusted his possessions to them. And to one he gave five talents, to another, two, and to another, one, each according to his own ability; and he went on his journey. Immediately the one who had received the five talents went and traded with them, and gained five more talents. In the same manner the one who had received the two talents gained two more. But he who received the one talent went away and dug in the ground, and hid his master's money. Now after a long time the master of those slaves came and settled accounts with them. And the one who had received the five talents came up and brought five more talents, saying, "Master, you entrusted five talents to me; see, I have gained five more talents." His master said to him, "Well done, good and faithful slave; you were faithful with a few things, I will put you in charge of many things, enter into the joy of your master." The one also who had received the two talents came up and said, "Master, you entrusted to me two talents; see, I have gained two more talents." His master said to him, "Well done, good and faithful slave; you were faithful with a few things, I will put you in charge of many things; enter into the joy of your master." And the one also who had received the one talent came up and said, "Master, I knew you to be a hard man, reaping where you did not sow, and gathering where you scattered no seed. And I was afraid, and went away and hid your talent in the ground; see, you have what is yours." But his master answered and said to him, "You wicked, lazy*

slave, you knew that I reap where I did not sow, and gather where I scattered no seed. Then you ought to have put my money in the bank, and on my arrival I would have received my money back with interest. Therefore take away the talent from him, and give it to the one who has the ten talents." For to everyone who has shall more be given, and he shall have an abundance; but from the one who does not have, even what he does have shall be taken away. And cast out the worthless slave into the outer darkness; in that place there shall be weeping and gnashing of teeth.

"A man...entrusted his possessions to them." They had control of the possessions; they had the use of them; they had legal rights over them; but in reality they were stewards, using things that didn't belong to them but were entrusted to them for a time. That speaks to me. What do we really own? My wife and I own an antique bookshelf that belonged to my grandparents. Grandma and Grandpa used it for a time, and now I have it. When I die the bookshelf will pass on to someone else. Things I "own" are only mine to be used for a certain period of time.

Jesus said, "No one can be My disciple who does not give up all his own possessions" (Luke 14:33). We really possess nothing -- not even our own lives -- because we ourselves have been "bought with a price" (1 Corinthians 6:20). Everything is on loan to us, even our breath. So we have a stewardship entrusted to us, to use things that aren't really ours.

"To one he gave five talents." How large were their responsibilities? One talent was 6000 denarii. Since one denarius was one day's wages, 6000 becomes 6000 days' wages, or what a person would earn in 24 years! Even the one-talent man received what a working person would earn in a lifetime, while the five-talent man was given five times as much. This gives us a hint of God's estimate of what He has given us to do!

"Each according to his own ability." Some have a greater capacity and more ability. It doesn't reflect on the person's heart or desire to serve, it simply means that their capacities are different. Our responsibilities are not all the same size.

"After a long time the master came and settled accounts with them." They had to give an account of what they had done with what they'd been given. With what you've been given, what have you done? It may be a long time before you settle accounts with your Master, but it will happen one day!

"Well done! (v.21) ... Well done! (v.23)" Both the two-talent and the five-talent persons received identical rewards! Each had achieved 100% increase. If we looked at their works based solely on outward results, we would think that one was twice as successful as the other. Let's say the increase is about how many people are in two pastors' churches: one had 400 and the other 1000. Or one manufacturer could turn out 4000 items a day while the other could make 10,000. One has only 40% of the results of the other. And in our limited way we look at the two and think that one is a greater person than the other, and we would expect that person to get a greater reward. But no, we are wrong: the master says identical words to each. When we can see what God sees, we will understand that each had achieved an increase of 100%. What we cannot see now is the initial capacities the master gave: what advantages, what kind of family life they had -- all the things the Lord can take into account that we cannot.

What we do is important. What we neglect is also important! The one-talent man is not reprimanded for something he did, but for what he failed to do! He buried his talent, twenty-four years of earnings not even drawing interest! He was held responsible for not doing the good that was in his power to do. We also have a responsibility to oppose evil when it is in our power to oppose. Doing nothing sometimes has terrible consequences.

Our reward will be determined not by the importance of our position or the magnitude of our responsibility, but by our faithfulness to the task, whatever it is. If the Lord has given us something small to do, He wants us to be faithful in doing that little thing. Sometimes I may think, "If I had a ministry like Joyce Meyers, I would really pray." Am I praying now, with my small responsibilities? If I had a ministry like Joyce Meyers, I would pray exactly as much as I do now, unless I retrain myself. If we are faithful in a little thing we will be faithful also in much, and vice-versa. The Lord doesn't have to give us big things to do to find out how we would do with big things! He can give us small responsibilities, and the way we respond to those is how we would respond to bigger ones.

Proverbs 20:6 A faithful man who can find?

Matthew 24:45-46 Who then is the faithful and sensible
slave whom his master put in charge of his household to
give them their food at the proper time? Blessed is that
slave whom his master finds so doing when he comes.

If we knew "the day" was tomorrow, would we have to hurry to do what we've left undone?

A friend of mine was a college football player named Lem Tucker, who told me his story. One summer day he and some friends were playing basketball outside when the suddenly the sun flared above them. They stopped playing and looked up to see a fireball heading toward earth. As the fireball came closer it formed into the shape of a cross, and in front of this cross of light they saw Jesus riding on a horse! Lem had been brought up attending church, so He knew exactly what was happening, but he also knew he wasn't ready, so he immediately dropped to his knees and asked God for another chance to be ready for Jesus' return. At that exact moment he woke up! Lem realized this was the second chance he prayed for, and right away he knelt beside the bed to repent and receive Jesus as his Savior.

The Law of Generosity

> *Matthew 7:1-5 Do not judge [krino: to condemn someone in our mind, to write them off, to think they are worthless, there is no hope for them, they're no good] lest you be judged. For in the way you judge, you will be judged; and by your standard of measure, it will be measured to you.*

Our standard of measure — of what? Of judgment! The measure of criticalness that we apply to others will be the same measure of criticalness that God applies to us.

> *(verse 3) And why do you look at the speck that is in your brother's eye, but do not notice the log that is in your own eye? Or how can you say to your brother, "Let me take the speck out of your eye," and behold, the log is in your own eye?*

Before I start to give out free advice, I need to look at myself. Before I think I should go and straighten out some person, I need to look in a mirror and ask, "What about me? Do I have the same problem I think I'm seeing in him?" I may be attempting to remove a speck from his life, when something bigger is in mine.

> *(verse 5) You hypocrite [you actor, you person behind a mask], first take the log out of your own eye, and then you will see clearly to take the speck out of your brother's eye.*

> *Luke 6:38 For whatever measure you deal out to others, it will be dealt to you in return.*

The Law of Generosity is that the strictness by which we will be judged [for rewards] will be determined by the mercy we've shown others. We determine the measure of mercy God will use when He tests our works! When our works are evaluated, the standard that is used will be determined by how we have been with other people. If we've been magnanimous and big-hearted, overlooking the faults of others, then when we approach Jesus that will be His attitude toward us. We may say, "Well Lord, I didn't do so well with such-and-such," and Jesus will say, "That's okay! You were big-hearted with other people and now I'm going to be big-hearted with you. You overlooked other people's faults, so I'm going to overlook yours." But if we were critical and held people to impossible standards, saying in our hearts, "This and this is wrong; if I were them I'd do it differently," then when we stand before the Lord, His attitude will be more like, "You were tough on others, and that forged the measure that I have to use for you; I'm going to as strict as you were as I examine your works." We can determine the size of the measure of mercy He uses toward the record of our works: a teaspoon, a cup, or a bucket of mercy.

> *James 2:12 So speak and so act, as those who are to be judged by the law of generosity [Gr. eleutheria: freedom, generosity, independence]. For judgment will be merciless to one who has shown no mercy; mercy triumphs over judgment.*

To translate *eleutheria* as "liberty" in this verse (as some translations do) didn't make much sense to me; the meaning of the verse remained a mystery. So I dug into the Greek and found that *eleutheria* can be translated as freedom, independence, or generosity. In context, "generosity" makes great sense. We could paraphrase "mercy triumphs over judgment" as "big-heartedness is stronger than criticalness." In a struggle between criticalness and big-heartedness, big-heartedness wins!

Matthew 5:7 Blessed are the merciful, for they shall receive mercy.

God loves mercy!

If you look up "endures forever" you'll find several things that occur once with it: God's goodness endures forever, His praise, judgments, name, dominion, and word. Twice the Bible says that "truth endures forever" and four times that "righteousness endures forever." How many times does the Bible declare "His mercy endures forever"? Forty-two times!

James 5:9 Do not complain, brethren, against one another, that you yourselves may not be judged; behold, the Judge is standing right at the door.

Mark 11:25 Forgive, if you have anything against anyone.

We aren't designed to bear the stress of harboring resentment and anger. This has consequences for our spiritual, mental, and physical wellbeing.

The law of generosity is crucial and will be one of the biggest factors in determining our reward in heaven. My prayer is that each one who reads this will receive a full reward! (2 John 1:8)

Endnotes, Chapter 11

[M] The parable of the wheat and the tares in Matthew13: 24-30, explained in Matthew 13:37-43, makes clear that when Jesus taught about the "kingdom", this kingdom includes both true and false Christians, i.e. some non-believers who mistakenly consider themselves Christians.

Chapter Twelve
Eternal Judgment of the Lost

A Final Judgment is Coming

In the last chapters we saw that not only those who believe in Jesus will be raised from the dead and receive a new body that will continue into eternity, but that the unrighteous dead will also be raised and receive an eternal body. What happens then? They will face a judgment of what they have done, as Hebrews 9:27 says, "inasmuch as it is appointed for men to die once and after this comes judgment."

How much do we understand of this judgment? Does God hold everyone to the same standard, or will He grade on a curve? How exacting will it be; will everything each person has done be scrutinized, or is God only concerned with the major things we've done?

The idea of a final judgment in which God holds people accountable for their lives is not a comfortable thought; in fact, it is a thought we try to avoid. Many would rather believe that God only threatens to punish. We hope that God is like Santa Claus, rumored to leave coal instead of presents if a child was bad, but does any child ever receive coal? Some people even scoff at the concept of judgment and joke about it. Someone once said to me, "I'm on my way to hell," and laughed! I was so shocked I didn't know what to say! I never tell jokes about hell, and if I hear one I usually say, "That's much too serious a subject to joke about."

If we want to be honest with the Scriptures, we have to hold on to the serious prospect that many people will be consigned to an eternity of punishment, sent away from the presence of God. God has provided a way of escape for them by sending His Son to suffer in their place but if they will not come to God for His answer, then their transgressions demand justice from God. John 3:36 "Whoever believes in the Son has eternal life, but whoever rejects the Son will not see life, for God's wrath remains on him."

> "Modern man's way is to turn a blind eye to all wrongdoing as long as he safely can. He tolerates it in others, feeling that there, but for the accident of circumstances, goes he. ...In our pagan way, we take it for granted that God feels as we do. The idea that retribution might be the moral law of God's world, and an expression of His holy character, seems to modern man quite fantastic: those who uphold it find themselves accused of projecting on to God their own pathological impulses of rage and vindictiveness. Yet the Bible insists throughout that this world which God in His goodness has made is a moral world, in which retribution is as basic a fact as breathing. God is the Judge of all the earth, and He will do right, vindicating the innocent, if such there be, but punishing (in the Bible phrase, 'visiting their sins upon') law-breakers (cf. Gen.18:25). God is not true to Himself unless He punishes sin. And unless one knows and feels the truth of this fact, that wrongdoers have no natural hope of anything from God but retributive judgment, one can never share the biblical faith in divine grace." (J.I. Packer, *Knowing God*, IVP 1973, p.118.)

Make no mistake that an ultimate judgment is coming. The Bible says that "God will bring every act to judgment" (Ecclesiastes 12:14).

Lesser Judgments Warn of the Ultimate Judgment

Small judgments from God, and some not-so-small, happen frequently. When Jesus was asked about one such incident, He saw it as a warning to all about the coming judgment.

> *Luke 13:1-5 Now on the same occasion there were some present who reported to Him about the Galileans, whose blood Pilate had mingled with their sacrifices. And He answered and said to them, "Do you suppose that these Galileans were greater sinners than all other Galileans, because they suffered this? I tell you, no, but, unless you repent, you will all likewise perish. Or do you suppose that those eighteen on whom the tower in Siloam fell and killed them, were worse culprits than all the men who live in Jerusalem? I tell you, no, but unless you repent, you will all likewise perish.*

Previous generations may have been more ready to understand calamities as warnings from God --as caution signs telling people to turn back because danger is ahead -- but our generation has become insensitive and superficial. In 1505 when Martin Luther was caught in a thunderstorm with lightning crashing all around, his instant response was, "Save me, Saint Anne, I'll become a monk." His close encounter turned his thoughts to eternity, and he did indeed become a monk, because that was seen as a more-sure way toward salvation. (After years of struggling to be sinless by his own effort, he finally came to the realization that justification is by grace. But would he have received the revelation of grace had he not started to seek God in the first place?) In contrast to Luther, a few years ago pro golfer Lee Trevino was nearly struck by lightning while playing in a tournament and reporters asked him what he had learned from the experience. "When the Almighty wants to play through, you let Him," the golfer quipped. (Non-golfers may not understand his words, "play through." Slower golfers will let faster golfers behind them "play through": the slower group stops playing and lets the faster group continue on.) Trevino's brush with death made him think of God, all right, but only as something to joke about!

As a generation, our sensitivity to spiritual things is dull. We seek materialistic explanations for tsunamis, droughts, plagues, etc.; we live in a material world and we think everything has a scientific answer. The Apostle Peter warned that at the end of the age, people would make fun of predictions of a coming judgment.

> *2 Peter 3:3-7 Know this first of all, that in the last days mockers will come with their mocking, following after their own lusts, and saying, "Where is the promise of His coming? For ever since the fathers fell asleep, all continues just as it was from the beginning of creation." For when they maintain this, it escapes their notice that ... (verse 6) the world at that time was destroyed, being flooded with water. But the present heavens and earth by His word are being reserved for fire, kept for the day of judgment and destruction of ungodly men.*

Noah's flood, according to the Bible, was brought on by lawlessness and wickedness so pervasive that God could find only one family worth sparing. It was the first warning of a universal judgment that is coming.

> *Genesis 6:5-6, 11-12 Then the Lord saw that the wickedness of man was great on the earth, and that every intent of the thoughts of his heart was only evil continually. And the Lord was sorry that He had made man on the earth, and He was grieved. ...(verse 11) Now the earth was corrupt in the sight of God, and the earth was filled with violence. And God looked on the earth, and behold, it was corrupt; for all flesh had corrupted their way upon the earth.*

Does this sound to you like it's describing the present? It does to me! We live with terrorism, gang violence, organized crime, "active shooter" tragedies, widespread corruption, mass starvation for the purpose of political power, ethnic cleansing, human trafficking, an epidemic of pedophilia, Ponzi schemes, and the trashing of the environment. How close are we to God's next universal judgment?

God's Attitude about Judgment

What will God's attitude be when the time for judgment comes? Will He rejoice? Will He enjoy it? I think the next verses shed light into what God feels about judgment.

> *Isaiah 28:21-22 For the Lord will rise up as at Mount Perazim,*
>
> *He will be stirred up as in the valley of Gibeon;*
>
> *To do His task, His unusual task*
>
> *[literally, His task is strange];*
>
> *And to work His work, His extraordinary work*
>
> *[lit., His work is alien].*
>
> *And now do not carry on as scoffers,*
>
> *Lest your fetters be made stronger;*
>
> *For I have heard from the Lord God of hosts,*
>
> *Of decisive destruction on all the earth.*

Isaiah prophesied about "decisive destruction on all the earth," and called it a strange task and an alien work. Judgment is called strange and alien to God, because it is so unlike His nature. It is like a meek man becoming extremely angry – it's possible for the meek person to do, but it is very unlike him.

> *2 Peter 3:9 The Lord is...not wishing for any to perish, but for all to come to repentance.*

> *Ezekiel 33:11 As surely as I live, declares the Sovereign Lord, I take no pleasure in the death of the wicked, but rather that they turn from their ways and live. Turn! Turn from you evil ways! Why will you die?*

Principles of God's Judgment

1) God's judgment will be exact.

In the last chapter we read of a time, described in the book of Revelation, in which books will be opened and the dead judged from what is recorded there. Let's review the "great white throne" judgment.

Revelation 20:11-13, 15 And I saw a great white throne and Him who sat upon it, from whose presence earth and heaven fled away, and no place was found for them. And I saw the dead, the great and the small, standing before the throne, and books were opened; and another book was opened, which is the book of life; and the dead were judged from the things which were written in the books, according to their deeds. And the sea gave up the dead which were in it, and death and Hades gave up the dead which were in them; and they were judged, every one according to their deeds. ...(verse 15) And if anyone's name was not found written in the book of life, he was thrown into the lake of fire.

I think we will be surprised at how exactingly the records will be reviewed. The Bible tells us that people's actions, words, and even motives will be scrutinized in that day. Not only what people did, but why they did it will be taken into account.

1 Peter 1:17 who impartially judges according to each man's work.

Matthew 12:36 And I say to you, that every careless word that men shall speak, they shall render account for it in the day of judgment.

1 Corinthians 4:5 Therefore do not go on passing judgment before the time, but wait until the Lord comes who will both bring to light the things hidden in the darkness and disclose the motives of men's hearts; and then each man's praise will come to him from God.

2) God's judgment will be totally impartial.

It won't matter who you are.

Romans 2:11 "For there is no partiality with God."

God's judgment will be exact, impartial, and according to the light given.

3) The strictness of the judgment will vary according to the light each person was given.

Matthew 11:20-24 Then he began to reproach the cities in which most of His miracles were done, because they did not repent. "Woe to you, Chorazin! Woe to you, Bethsaida! For if the miracles had occurred in Tyre and Sidon which occurred in you, they would have repented long ago in sackcloth and ashes. Nevertheless I say to you, it shall be more tolerable for Tyre and Sidon in the day of judgment, than for you. And you, Capernaum ...if the miracles had occurred in Sodom which occurred in you, it would have remained to this day. Nevertheless I say to you that it shall be more tolerable for the land of Sodom in the day of judgment, than for you."

Luke 12:47-48 And that slave who knew his master's will and did not get ready or act in accord with his will, shall receive many lashes, but the one who did not know it, and committed deeds worthy of a flogging, will receive but few. And from everyone who has been given much shall much be required; and to whom they entrusted much, of him they will ask all the more.

One Common Misunderstanding: The Intermediate versus the Eternal State of the Unrighteous Dead

Two Greek words distinguish between the intermediate state and the eternal state of the unrighteous dead: *Hades* and *Gehenna*, (also called the "lake of fire"). In English, both Hades and Gehenna are translated "hell."

Hades (probably from *hado*, "all-receding") is the intermediate state of the unrighteous dead.

> *Revelation 20:13-14 And death and Hades gave up the dead which were in them ... And death and Hades were thrown into the lake of fire. This is the second death, the lake of fire.*

Thus Hades is a temporary existence, not an eternal one. What ultimately happens to Hades? Hades gives up its dead, then Hades itself is thrown into the lake of fire.

Gehenna (Heb.: Valley of Hinnom) is the eternal state of the unrighteous dead. Gehenna was a deep, narrow ravine south of Jerusalem where at one point in history the Jews had offered their children to Moloch (2 Kings 23:10). Later it became a garbage-heap with continual fires burning. Jesus used this place of waste and burning as a graphic image of the place of eternal punishment. So Gehenna is another name for the lake of fire.

> *Matthew 5:29 And if your right eye makes you stumble, cut it off, and throw it from you; for it is better for you that one of the parts of your body perish, than for your whole body to go into Gehenna.*

> *Mark 9:47-48 And if your eye causes you to stumble, cast it out; it is better for you to enter the kingdom of God with one eye, than having two eyes, to be cast into Gehenna, WHERE THEIR WORM DOES NOT DIE, AND THE FIRE IS NOT QUENCHED.*

As we've seen, at the Great White Throne the dead are brought up from Hades, then condemned to the Lake of Fire. Thus, when an unsaved person dies his body stays on earth and his soul goes to Hades until the resurrection of the unrighteous. At that resurrection his soul and body stand before God for judgment, after which both his soul and body will be sent into the Lake of Fire. We can compare it to a prisoner being held in jail until his trial, standing before the judge, and then being sent to prison.

Puzzling Passages

Now we come to a few more very intriguing passages that have to do with hell. Some are puzzling (I should probably stop right here!) and my interpretation may be too literal; search it out yourself to see what you think.

> *Ephesians 4:8-9 WHEN HE ASCENDED ON HIGH, HE LED CAPTIVE A HOST OF CAPTIVES, AND HE GAVE GIFTS TO MEN. Now this expression, "He ascended," what does it mean except that He also had descended into the lower parts of the earth?*

> *1 Peter 4:6 For the gospel has for this purpose been preached even to those who are dead, that though they are judged in the flesh as men, they may live in the spirit according to the will of God.*

What a strange expression, that the gospel has been "preached to those who are dead"! The purpose of the preaching was that the dead could live, the passage says. The question we come to is what did God do with the Old Testament believers? When I say "believers," I'm speaking of those people Hebrews 11:39-40 refers to when it says that some people who lived before Jesus came, gained approval through their faith: "And all these having gained approval through their faith, did not receive what was promised, because God had provided something better for us, so that apart from us they should not be made perfect." They had faith in as much of God as He had revealed to them. Legally, they had no right to go to heaven because the blood of Jesus had not yet been shed. (The Old Testament offerings, which helped them partially understand, were a prediction of what Jesus would do; until He actually did it they could not go to heaven.)

So here's my take on this unusual passage. Peter tells us that Jesus went and preached to the Old Testament believers after they were dead, and starting with what they had believed in part, He unveiled the fulfillment of it, so they could believe in Him and live. And Ephesians picks up the thread to say that when Jesus ascended to heaven, He took them with Him.

Where were they in the meantime? I think Luke 16 tells us that they were in the same place Jesus referred to when He said to the thief on the cross, "This day you shall be with Me in Paradise." That day the thief went to Paradise and was with Jesus' spirit there while at the same time Jesus' body was in the tomb and Jesus' soul was suffering in hell! Now I admit this may be stretching things too far, but read Luke 16:19-31 to see if you agree. So these places, Hades and Paradise, were separated from one another; on one side were the righteous dead with Abraham, and on the other side the unrighteous dead in Hades. When Jesus ascended, He emptied Paradise of all the Old Testament believers and took them to heaven with Him. And we should add, as the man laments that if only someone would return from the dead to tell his relatives, that Someone <u>has</u> come from the dead: His name is Jesus! He came to persuade all men, leaving no every excuse for those who refuse to respond.

As uncomfortable as the concept of hell is for us, Jesus Himself spoke about it. So we have to take it as a terrible reality, as the rich man in Luke 16 says, "I am in agony here." May we let its solemn reality spur us on so we don't waste our time or waste our lives, but do all we can to "save others, snatching them out of the fire" (Jude 23)!

Chapter Thirteen
Jesus' Suffering in Hell

Images of Hell and Jesus' Suffering

The New Testament does not say much about what Jesus was experiencing while his body was in the tomb. We do know that Jesus went to Hades because of

Revelation 1:18 "I was dead, and behold, I am alive forevermore, and I have the keys of death and of Hades."

Specifically we learn that it was his soul that went to Hades.

Acts 2:27 "BECAUSE THOU WILT NOT ABANDON MY SOUL TO HADES."

And we learn from the New Testament that death for Jesus contained agony, and that this agony did not end until his resurrection. Acts 2:24 "But God raised Him up again, putting an end to the agony of death, since it was impossible for Him to be held in its power." Some interpret the Bible to say that Jesus did not suffer while dead but was in Paradise being comforted. This scripture seems to contradict that idea.

Do we know anything more than just this much?

I believe that in the Psalms we have different images of hell, and that these images of hell actually give us prophetic foreshadowings of Jesus' experiences in hell. Think of a "foreshadowing" like this: imagine you are on a street near the corner of a building, with late afternoon sun casting the long shadow of the building over you. Someone is walking beside the building out of your sight with the sun behind them, and you can see their shadow approaching because it has come past the corner before they have. If you closely examine the shadow you may learn that they are carrying a briefcase, wearing pants and a sport coat, etc. Their shadow is a "prophecy," even though somewhat dark and vague, of what is about to come into view when the person passes the corner of the building and comes into view.

By understanding certain passages as foreshadowings, there is mutual agreement that certain psalms are prophetic of the physical sufferings of the Messiah. In Psalm 22, for instance. "My God, my God, why hast Thou forsaken me?... My bones are out of joint. ... They look, they stare at me; They divide my garments among them, And for my clothing they cast lots," etc. This psalm is quoted by the New Testament writers more than any other Old Testament passage, and is interpreted by the New Testament as predicting Jesus' sufferings on the cross. In it, David prophetically spoke about experiences he did not have, experiences which in fact go far beyond anything David experienced. As a prophet of God, David predicted the sufferings of the Messiah on the cross, centuries before the event.

In a similar way, I think that other psalms prophetically speak to us which focus on the big picture of the cross and resurrection, in which we hear the Messiah retelling the whole history of His dying, suffering, and being released from that suffering. Let's listen to Psalm 116 as if we are hearing Jesus retelling the story after it is complete, and see if it doesn't make perfect sense. Imagine these as words in which Jesus retells His experience:

Psalm 116:3-4, 6b-10

3 The cords of death encompassed me

And the terrors of Sheol came upon me;

I found distress and sorrow.

4 Then I called upon the name of the Lord:

"O Lord, I beseech You, deliver my soul!" ...

6b I was brought low, and He saved me.

7 Return to your rest, O my soul,

For the Lord has dealt bountifully with you.

8 For You have rescued my soul from death,

My eyes from tears,

My feet from stumbling

9 I shall walk before the Lord in the land of the living

10 I believed when I said, "I am greatly afflicted."

Then we come across some psalms that I believe reveal the sufferings of the Messiah after death and before resurrection, in which He speaks from the midst of that experience. Certain psalms and other passages are prophetic of Jesus' sufferings in hell; please tread softly and reverently as you consider these next passages. We turn now to the psalm quoted second-most often in the New Testament: listen to the next few quotes and see if they sound like Jesus' thoughts coming to us from the middle of hell.

Psalm 69:2-4 & 14-15

2 I have sunk in deep mire, and there is no foothold;

I have come into deep waters and a flood overwhelms me.

3 I am weary with my crying; my throat is parched;

My eyes fail while I wait for my God.

4 Those who hate me without a cause are more than the hairs of my head;

Those who would destroy me are powerful. ...

14 Deliver me from the mire, and do not let me sink;

May I be delivered from my foes, and from the deep waters.

15 May the flood of water not overflow me,

And may the deep not swallow me up,

And may the pit not shut its mouth on me.

What is the image of hell that is given here; what does it feel like to be in hell? It feels like sinking in quicksand -- like drowning -- like falling down and being trapped in a narrow pit. There are so many images, it makes me think that what these verses are trying to describe for us is the inner experience of hell, that is, the emotions of someone who is in hell.

When I was seven years old I nearly drowned. I had not yet learned to swim and was floating on an inner tube in a lake at Chapman Dam. I realized I was getting too far from shore and jumped off to pull the inner tube closer, but the water was much deeper than I thought, and down I went into water over my head. I can still picture the dark donut shape of the inner-tube way over my head, jumping but not being able to reach it, and the panic I felt as I breathed in water. Just then our neighbor, Marge Brennan, snatched me up -- she had seen me jump off and go under. Have you come close to drowning? (When I ask a group of people this question, I'm always surprised at how many have, usually it's about one-fourth of the audience!) The sense of panic that we experienced while breathing in water is a taste of hell.

Or if you had fallen down a well, and looking up could see a little patch of light, but it seems like the mouth of the well is closing off – that's what hell feels like.

> *Psalm 40:2 "He brought me up out of the pit of destruction,*
> *out of the miry clay; And He set my feet upon a rock*
> *making my footsteps firm."*

These could be Jesus' words as He tells the experience He had. It felt like being in slimy mud down in the bottom of a pit, with no solid foothold. Imagine the panic of gradually sinking with no way to climb out!

Psalm 88:6-7

6 Thou has put me in the lowest pit, in dark places, in the depths.

7 Thy wrath has rested upon me, and Thou hast afflicted me with all Thy waves. Selah.

"All Thy waves" are God's wrath against sin, coming against Jesus' soul in wave after wave. He had to endure every wave until the last of God's anger against the last sin was absorbed. Just think of the little that you know of the horrible things people have done to each other, and how it can make you angry. God's wrath against all that we know about, and all the wickedness we don't know about, had to be suffered by Jesus' soul. He suffered for all the wicked things you've done, and that I've done. To die physically was not enough to satisfy the judgment of God, because the penalty of sin is not just death but the wrath of God. And until that last wrath of God was expended, Jesus stayed to suffer.

Psalm 88:8, 14-18

8 Thou hast removed my acquaintances far from me;

Thou hast made me an object of loathing to them;

I am shut up and cannot go out. ...

14 O Lord, why dost Thou reject my soul?

Why dost Thou hide Thy face from me?

15 I was afflicted and about to die from my youth on;

I suffer Thy terrors; I am overcome.

16 Thy burning anger has passed over me;

Thy terrors have destroyed me.

17 They have surrounded me like water all day long;

They have encompassed me altogether.

18 Thou hast removed lover and friend far from me;

My acquaintances are darkness.

Next we turn to the prophet Jonah. Jonah's experience of being in a fish or whale is spoken of in the New Testament as prophetic of what the Son of Man would experience. As we look at Jonah's words we will recognize them as telling about Jesus' suffering in hell, and also some hints about how Jesus' victory started right there.

Jonah 2:1-9

Then Jonah prayed to the Lord his God from the stomach of the fish,

2 and he said, "I called out of my distress to the Lord, and He answered me.

I cried for help from the depth of Sheol; Thou didst hear my voice.

3 For Thou hadst cast me into the deep, into the heart of the seas,

And the current engulfed me.

All Thy breakers and billows passed over me.

[For Jonah the breakers were physical waves; for Jesus they were the wrath of God.]

4 So I said, 'I have been expelled from Thy sight.

Nevertheless I will look again toward Thy holy temple.'

5 Water encompassed me to the point of death, the great deep engulfed me,

Weeds were wrapped around my head.

6 I descended to the roots of the mountains.

The earth with its bars was around me forever,

As terrible as Jonah's experience was, do you see how what he tells about goes further than what Jonah suffered? Jonah wasn't surrounded by the earth with its bars, but Jesus was. Jonah wasn't in Sheol (the place of the dead), but Jesus was. So Jonah prophesied of experiences beyond his own.

> *But Thou hast brought up my life from the pit, O Lord my God.*
>
> *7 While I was fainting away, I remembered the Lord;*
>
> *And my prayer came to Thee, into Thy holy temple.*
>
> *8 Those who regard vain idols forsake their faithfulness,*
>
> *9 But I will sacrifice to Thee with the voice of thanksgiving.*
>
> *That which I have vowed I will pay. Salvation is from the Lord."*

Jonah said, "While I was fainting away, I remembered the Lord," and talked about offering a sacrifice of thanks. When does giving thanks become a <u>sacrifice</u> of thanks? When the person does not feel thankful. When you think about it, how could someone be expected to thank God after being swallowed by a whale? Can a person thank God in the middle of circumstances that are uncomfortable, hurtful, or even life-threatening? But Jonah did; he began to thank God from inside the fish/whale. So here is the sequence: he was fainting away – he remembered the Lord – he began to give thanks, even though he didn't feel like it.

The next reference picks up the narrative and goes into more detail for us.

> *Lamentations 3*
>
> *1 I am the man who has seen affliction because of the rod of His wrath. ...*
>
> *6 In dark places He has made me dwell, like those who have long been dead.*
>
> *7 He has walled me in so that I cannot go out; He has made my chain heavy.*
>
> *8 Even when I cry out and call for help, He shuts out my prayer. ...*

15 He has filled me with bitterness, He has made me drunk with wormwood.

16 And He has broken my teeth with gravel; He has made me cower in the dust.

This is not describing the physical suffering of Jesus --whose teeth were not broken, etc.-- but it is describing the suffering of His soul in physical terms that we can relate to. To engage us, to make sense to us, it has to be expressed in these physical terms.

17 And my soul has been rejected from peace; I have forgotten happiness.

18 So I say, "My strength has perished, and so has my hope from the Lord."

We reach the absolute lowest point of Jesus' suffering. At this moment, Jesus gave up hope, He felt like He would never get out of hell, and thought He would never escape. Hope faded, then extinguished. He gave up. He thought things would never be different and resigned Himself to continue to exist like this, forever.

But then, something happened.

19 Remember my affliction and my wandering, the wormwood and bitterness.

20 Surely my soul remembers and is bowed down within me.

21 This I recall to mind, therefore I have hope.

Hope returns. (Remember how Psalm 116 linked recognizing His affliction with believing? See Psalm 116:10. This is a fuller description.)

22 The Lord's lovingkindnesses indeed never cease, for His compassions never fail.

23 They are new every morning; great is Thy faithfulness.

24 "The Lord is my portion," says my soul, "therefore I have hope in Him."

This corresponds to Jonah's "while I was fainting away, I remembered the Lord," expanded for us into actual thoughts. What was it that made the difference? When Jesus was at His lowest point, what began to pull Him through? The crucial difference, the thing that turned it around for Him, was what He knew about the character of His Father. That's what rekindled hope where there was none. And I think it's the same for us. When we get to a really low point, when we get to a really desperate situation – when we feel all alone and abandoned – the thing that will pull us through is the deep heart-knowledge we have of the character of God. Is God good, or not?

Jesus in hell begins to remember what His Father is like, and says to Himself, 'Wait a minute! The Father does not afflict for nothing; He does not afflict willingly; He is not like that.' Lamentations goes on:

25 The Lord is good to those who wait for Him, to the person who seeks Him.

26 It is good that he waits silently for the salvation of the Lord.

What is He doing? Giving thanks. Specifically, offering a "sacrifice of thanksgiving." In the midst of this horrendous trial, far worse than anything any of us will ever go through or have to face, Jesus begins to say, 'This is good. It's good.'

27 It is good for a man that he should bear the yoke in his youth.

'Thank you, Father, that I am doing this.'

28 Let him sit alone and be silent since He has laid it on him.

29 Let him put his mouth in the dust, perhaps there is hope.

30 Let him give his cheek to the smiter; let him be filled with reproach.

31 For the Lord will not reject forever,

32 For if He causes grief, then He will have compassion

According to His abundant lovingkindness.

33 For He does not afflict willingly or grieve the sons of men.

So this knowledge of His Father gives Him a reason to have hope and to give thanks, and He begins to win the victory in the midst of hell. How did victory start? By giving thanks. Thanks for who God is — and for the experience. Isaiah said that He would see the <u>result</u> of the travail of his soul and be satisfied (Isaiah 53:11). It's awesome to realize that the satisfaction began right in hell. Jesus is remembering the purpose for it all – "if He causes grief, then He will have compassion" – the grief that God caused Jesus allows His compassion to flow to the rest of mankind. And what was the start of the victory? Jesus remembered that God never does anything without a purpose.

Sometimes when we are in troubling times we give God thanks for other things and we can give Him thanks for who He is, but have we learned the secret of thanking God for the hard time itself? That's when victory begins to be released! Often we have to win the internal victory while our trial is still going on, and then the external deliverance can be set in motion. Win the victory where you are, and let God arrange the circumstances after that.

Some of us have suffered in the past and some are suffering right now. Some of you are suffering in ways I never have. But Jesus knows. He has suffered more than any, and He knows exactly what it's like. If He could offer thanks when He didn't feel like it, from the middle of the terrors of hell – if in those feelings He could begin to thank God, then He can give us the strength to begin to offer our own sacrifice of thanksgiving. Even if you are at the point of fainting away, it's not too late. Begin to thank God. This has a purpose. God never does anything for nothing, and He doesn't enjoy afflicting us; His character is such that we know this is true. Thank Him now and release His power to do what He wants to in your situation.

Next we come to Psalm 18, which I interpret as another rehearsal by Jesus after the whole experience of going to hell and being released from there. And I have a favorite setting – it may be fanciful or factual, I have no way of knowing – in which I think of Jesus saying these words. In the Gospel of John we have the record that when John himself came into the empty tomb, he believed. He draws our attention to the head covering folded up by itself, as if this had special significance for John (see John 20:4-8).

Finding Himself back in His body, now gloriously transformed, coming suddenly from a place of torment into a place of joy, Jesus sat on the rock bench of the tomb and collected His thoughts. As He sat there He folded up this piece of cloth. Maybe John had seen Jesus do this other times (folding a cloth after dinner, perhaps), because somehow John recognized Jesus' handiwork when he saw the cloth. So I like to think of the next psalm as expressing the thoughts that went through Jesus' mind as He was sitting there and folding up the cloth.

Psalm 18

1 I love Thee, O Lord, my strength.

2 The Lord is my rock and my fortress and my deliverer,

   My God, my rock, in whom I take refuge;

   My shield and the horn of my salvation, my stronghold.

3 I call upon the Lord, who is worthy to be praised, and I am saved from my enemies.

4 The cords of death encompassed me, and the torrents of ungodliness terrified me.

5 The cords of Sheol surrounded me; the snares of death confronted me.

6 In my distress I called upon the Lord, and cried to my God for help;

   He heard my voice out of His temple,

And my cry for help before Him came into His ears.

7 Then the earth shook and quaked;

And the foundations of the mountains were trembling and were shaken,

Because He was angry.

8 Smoke went up out of His nostrils, and fire from His mouth devoured;

Coals were kindled by it.

9 He bowed the heavens also, and came down with thick darkness under His feet.

10 And He rode upon a cherub and flew; and He sped upon the wings of the wind. ...

16 He sent from on high, He took me; He drew me out of many waters.

17 He delivered me from my strong enemy,

And from those who hated me, for they were too mighty for me.

18 They confronted me in the day of my calamity, But the Lord was my stay.

19 He brought me forth also into a broad place;

He rescued me, because He delighted in me.

Chapter Fourteen
Eternal Security

Many sincere Christians worry about losing their salvation after they have been saved. Some know that they are saved right now, but worry that something may happen in the future that will make them fall away. Some think they get "saved" and "lost" day by day depending on how they are doing in their struggle against sin. Still others are in the worst condition of all: they tried to live a holy life but found it impossible, gave up and have concluded that there is no hope for them and think they are on their way to hell. What a shame that true Christians would think they are doomed to hell! My heart goes out to them and to all who worry about losing their salvation. This chapter seeks to convince you that once you are truly saved, it is impossible for you to lose your salvation.

As we approach it, we should remember that this controversy has gone on for centuries and that sincere Bible scholars have opinions on each side of the debate. Whole denominations come down on one side or the other of this question. There is obviously much confusion, and we have to be honest that "rightly dividing the word" (2 Timothy 2:15) is not always easy. A dose of humility about our own opinion might not be a bad place to start. Having said this, I'm going to present as strong a case as I can for what I believe to be true.

As further preparation to approaching this subject, let's make a commitment to accept other Christians no matter what they conclude concerning this doctrine. The only eternal division is between believers and unbelievers, between light and darkness (2 Corinthians 6:14-15). The line between those who believe you can lose your salvation and those who believe you cannot is not a dividing line for fellowship! Whatever you conclude about this doctrine, it is no reason to avoid Christians who believe differently.

Let's begin with a brief review. What part of salvation is involved in our eternal life? Our initial salvation -- justification. There are many scriptures about salvation, some of which deal with the on-going work of salvation (sanctification), some of which speak of a salvation that hasn't come to us yet (glorification), and some that speak of salvation as a completed action in the past (justification). Entrance to heaven depends on justification alone, which is what we are talking about when we talk about eternal security. ((If you haven't read the chapter on the three parts of salvation, it contains important preparation for what follows.))

After presenting a few main arguments in favor of eternal security – that once a person has been justified, he or she cannot lose that justification – we'll go on in the next chapter to discuss some scriptures that seem to speak against this position. But first enjoy these simple truths and let them sink into your soul!

A Person Can Know that He Has Eternal Life

> *1 John 5:13 These things I have written to you who believe in the name of the Son of God, in order that you may know that you have eternal life.*

The Apostle John tells us plainly that God wants us to know that we have eternal life. Read what the plain language is: "you have eternal life." "Have" is in the present tense: you have it already. Eternal life is not something that begins when you die, but something that began the moment you put your trust in Jesus. Isn't it marvelous? "That you may know – that you have – eternal life." God wants us to be in no doubt about it. How can anyone know, if the possibility exists they may be lost in the future?

A few decades ago it was unfashionable to "know" you were saved; it was looked on as presumptuous. The "spiritual" attitude to take, it was taught, was to hang your head and say, "Well, I hope I'm saved. I sure am trying, but I'll just have to wait until I'm at heaven's gate to find out." That was seen as more humble. But what a shallow understanding of justification this reveals! And do you see how it dishonors Jesus, as if what He did is not enough or what He promised is not enough for us to be sure?

Jesus is Able to Keep Us

> *2 Timothy 1:12 for I know whom I have believed and am convinced that He is able to keep [guard] what I have entrusted to Him until that day.*
>
> *2 Timothy 4:18 The Lord will...bring me safely to His heavenly kingdom.*

Have you committed your salvation to His keeping? Then He is well able to guard it. What do these verses mean if not that true Christians are eternally secure? Are we to believe that we have Jesus guarding us, but that is not enough? Is there some better Shepherd? Is the wolf really stronger than He is?

Or maybe you relied on Jesus to save you initially, but now you think you must rely on yourself to hold on to salvation? If that is how God set it up, you have a right to be proud when you enter heaven as you say, "Jesus saved me, but I hung on; I kept myself from falling." No, Jesus is the Savior and the Keeper of our salvation. Paul just told us that he knew whom he had believed and had become convinced of Jesus' keeping ability.

> "The moment you open yourself to Christ, God gets a 'beachhead' in your life. ...Once Christ is given a beachhead, he begins the campaign to take over more and more territory until all of your life is completely his. There will be struggles and battles, but the outcome will never be in

doubt. God has promised that 'he who began a good work in you will carry it on to completion.'" (Rick Warren, *The Purpose-Driven Life*, Zondervan 2002, p.218.)

> *John 6:37-40 All that the Father gives Me shall come to Me, and the one who comes to Me I will certainly not cast out. For I have come down from heaven, not to do My own will, but the will of Him who sent Me. And this is the will of Him who sent Me, that of all that He has given Me I lose nothing, but raise it up on the last day. For this is the will of My Father, that everyone who beholds the Son and believes in Him, may have eternal life; and I Myself will raise him up on the last day.*

Another irrefutable scripture! (People who argue against eternal security usually begin their argument with a verse that is questionable in its interpretation, never with something as straightforward as this. But if eternal security is incorrect, then they have to find a way to explain their way around these straightforward scriptures!) According to John 6, if once-saved people were lost, Jesus would fail in doing His Father's will. The Father's will is that He "lose nothing." If even one justified person is lost after being saved, then Jesus has failed to do the Father's will. This will never happen! The doctrine of eternal insecurity dishonors the Savior, who will never fail in doing His Father's will.

> *John 10:27-28 My sheep hear My voice, and I know them, and they follow Me, and I give eternal life to them, and they shall never perish; and no one shall snatch them out of My hand.*

This reads plainly. "No one shall snatch them out of My hand." "They shall never perish." "'Never' can only mean 'never,' wrote Dr. Francis Schaeffer (*25 Basic Bible Studies*, Crossway Books 1996, p.88). According to John 10, who can snatch us from God's hand? No one. "Oh, but," someone says, "no one <u>else</u> can snatch you, but you can jump out." Did it say "no one else," or "no one"? You had to insert "else" into the verse; are you comfortable adding to the Scriptures? The plain meaning is that "no one" includes you, which is confirmed by a similar passage,

> *Romans 8:38-39 "For I am convinced that neither death, nor life, nor angels, nor principalities, nor things present, nor things to come, nor powers, nor height, nor depth, nor any other created thing, shall be able to separate us from the love of God, which is in Christ Jesus our Lord."*

If someone went to hell it surely would mean that he was separated from the love of God, yet Paul declares that nothing can separate us (believers) from that love, even "things to come" [what we may fear we may do in the future] or "any other created thing." Are you a created thing? Yes. Then not even you can separate yourself from His love.

Jesus is able to keep us. Jesus loses nothing. No one is strong enough to snatch us away from the Good Shepherd.

These scriptures are clear. Often our mistake is that we let things that we are having trouble understanding cast their haze over the things that are already clear to us. Hold on to what's clear, and let the Lord bring light to the confusing passages.

True Believers are not even Judged in the Future about Eternal Life!

> *John 3:18 He who believes in Him is not judged.*

> *John 5:24 Truly, truly, I say to you, he who hears My word, and believes Him who sent Me, has eternal life, and does not come into judgment, but has passed out of death into life.*

> "The life that is given at salvation to believers is the promise of eternal life (*aionios zoe*). *Aionios* means that which is not temporal, cannot be lost, nor

destroyed." (Spiros Zodhiates, *The Complete Word Study New Testament*, AMG 1999, p.582.)

Jesus Himself told us that if we hear His word and believe, we have eternal life, a life that cannot be lost or destroyed, according to the meaning of aionios. (For an example of the contrast between eternal and temporal, look up 2 Corinthians 4:17-18). Because we have eternal life, we do not come into judgment, but have <u>already</u> passed out of death into life. Can you believe how good this news is? We who have been justified by His blood will not face a judgment of whether or not we are going to heaven; it was already decided when we put our faith in Jesus! We passed from death to life! How dare anyone say, then, that we will pass from life back to death? Jesus said we would not be judged.

Salvation is a Gift, and God's Gifts are Irrevocable

Ephesians 2:8 For by grace you have been saved thru faith; it is the gift of God.

Romans 11:29 For the gifts and callings of God are irrevocable.

Ecclesiastes 3:14 Everything God does will remain forever.

If justification is a gift, and gifts are irrevocable, then justification is irrevocable. Anything irrevocable cannot be rescinded or taken back. God gives the gift of salvation (justification), and has made it an irrevocable gift.

Those who are Told to Depart, Never Knew Him

Jesus gave a sobering warning to those who deceive themselves, thinking they are Christians when in fact they have never known Him or done His will. But notice that in this warning He said, "I never knew you," not "I once knew you, but now I don't."

> Matthew 7:22-23 *Many will say to Me on that day, "Lord, Lord, did we not prophesy in Your name, and in Your name cast out demons, and in Your name perform many miracles?" And then I will declare to them, "I never knew you; depart from Me, you who practice lawlessness."*

At the same time, we need to pay close attention to Jesus' warning here: some of us who think we are saved, are not! Just because I attend worship services, observe certain rituals, or have been baptized does not mean that I am a genuine Christian. I may know much about God without having a relationship with Him. 2 Peter 2:20-23 tells us that there will even be false teachers among us, who have escaped certain corrupt behaviors by their knowledge about Jesus – they have become washed pigs, but nevertheless are still pigs or dogs at heart – they have an outward form of godliness, but no inward change. Many people will be surprised at the judgment to discover that He never knew them, and they never knew Him; a real relationship with God was absent. The Bible tells us to examine ourselves to see if we are truly in the faith: 2 Corinthians 13:5 "Test yourselves if you are in the faith; examine yourselves! Or do you not recognize this about yourselves, that Jesus Christ is in you—unless indeed you fail the test?"

> "Paul knows that true Christian faith is the beginning of a life which, given by God, will be brought to completion by him (Phil.1:6). He also knows that genuine faith is seen in patient and steadfast day-to-day Christian living, while counterfeit faith, so hard in its early stages to distinguish from the real thing, withers and dies." (N.T. Wright, *Tyndale New Testament Commentaries, Colossians and Philemon*, IVP 1997, p.83.)

You probably know people who at one time were involved in Christian activities and a Christian life-style but today are not. What can we say to them? If, because of our doctrine of eternal security, we assure them that they are saved no matter what their present behavior is or how much sin they are involved in, we could be giving them false assurance! I like Dr. Wright's statement above that genuine conversion and counterfeit faith are hard to distinguish in the early stages, so perhaps the people weren't really saved in the first place. Be careful not to use your understanding of eternal security as a false comfort for those who may need to be converted.

Disobedient Christians will be Disciplined, but not Rejected

> *Psalm 89:30-34 If his sons forsake My law, and do not walk in My judgments, if they violate My statutes, and do not keep my commandments, then I will visit their transgression with the rod, and their iniquity with stripes. But I will not break off My lovingkindness from him, nor deal falsely in My faithfulness. My covenant I will not violate, nor will I alter the utterance of My lips.*

Jesus Saves Forever

> *Hebrews 7:24-25 But He, on the other hand, because He abides forever, holds His priesthood permanently. Hence also He is able to save forever those who draw near to God through Him, since He always lives to make intercession for them.*

>"The ground of our salvation is not our good works in the past, present, or future, but the perfect work of Christ. ... The Lord saves us both completely and forever. The Christian could be lost again only if Christ failed as priest." (Francis Schaeffer, *25 Basic Bible Studies*, Crossway Books 1996, p.87.)

Chapter Fifteen

Questions Regarding Eternal Security

Let's continue by discussing scriptures that seem to argue the other side, i.e. that salvation can be lost. By looking at some of these, we'll see how easy it is to become confused and to question the clear pronounce-ments we just considered. Hopefully we'll cover enough passages that throw doubt on the issue of eternal security that you will be persuaded that there are good answers for any that are not addressed here. (At the same time, I often wonder at the lack of objectivity of those who embrace a "pet scripture" that proves the saved-again-lost-again position to them, who disregard and have no answer for the ironclad passages we discussed in the last chapter!)

How Things Get Misunderstood

•Confusing the Greek Tenses for Salvation

Much of the security/insecurity confusion clears up when we begin to be careful with the distinctions in the Greek tenses of verbs.

> *1 Corinthians 15:1-2 Now I would remind you, brothers, of the gospel I preached to you, which you received, in which you stand, (verse 2) and by which you are being saved, if you hold fast to the word I preached to you – unless you believed in vain. (English Standard Version)*

Verse one is plain to us that it is speaking about our justification: the gospel was preached, you received it and stand in it. But in verse 2 confusion comes in with the phrase "if you hold fast." Some interpret this as applying to what has already been stated, to verse one. But it is better interpreted it as applying only to the phrase immediately before: "you are being saved if you hold fast." (Some English translations say "are saved" and others "are being saved.") The Greek tense in verse 2 is the present indicative, and "the present indicative asserts something which is occurring while the speaker is making the statement" (Spiros Zodhiates, *The Complete Word Study New Testament*, AMG 1999, p.857). So the first verse speaks of justification, and the second of sanctification. We are (presently) being saved (sanctified) if we hold fast; if we do not hold fast, we can lose ground in this area of sanctification. How does this relate to the gospel? We should remember that the gospel includes the good news of justification, that Jesus died instead of me for my forgiveness, and the good news that Jesus now lives instead of me for my sanctification. Being careful with the Greek tenses, we should interpret "received" in a past tense, and "are being saved" in the present. But then, as if there hasn't been enough confusion, Paul thinks of one more possibility: that the person "believed in vain," i.e. was never genuinely converted and gave only intellectual assent to the gospel they heard but never a heart commitment (which we discussed previously). This scripture covers it all!

Here is another scripture in which the verb tenses help clear away confusion:

> *Philippians 2:12-13 So then, my beloved, just as you have always obeyed, ... work out your salvation with fear and trembling; for it is God who is at work in you, both to will and to work for His good pleasure.*

What type of salvation is Paul talking about here? Past, present, or future? Present – therefore, sanctification. We do not "work out" our justification (you don't work for a gift), but we do work out our sanctification "with fear and trembling."

In chapter 5 you already saw this last example of the aorist tense being used for the initial, once-for-all-time justification of the Christian while the present tense is used to describe the ongoing sanctification process, but it's worth repeating. In the next verses, "having been firmly rooted" refers to justification, while "now being built up" refers to sanctification.

> *Colossians 2:6-7 As you therefore have received Christ Jesus the Lord, so walk in Him, having been firmly rooted and now being built up in Him and established in your faith.*

> "It is particularly worth noting that, whereas 'rooted' is an aorist, indicating a once-for-all planting of the Christian 'in' Christ, 'built up' is in the present, suggesting continual growth." (N.T. Wright, *Tyndale New Testament Commentaries, Colossians and Philemon*, IVP 1997, p.99.)

•Arguing from Silence to Make the Text Say More than It Says

> *Revelation 3:5 He who overcomes shall thus be clothed in white garments; and I will not erase his name from the book of life.*

It's easy to read between the lines and suppose that the opposite is true; that he who does not overcome will have his name erased. But is this what the text says, or is that an argument from silence? The verse is a lovely promise meant to reassure us that erasure will not happen, yet it gets twisted into something that engenders fear. We quickly get in trouble when we make the Bible say what it does not! If you want further confirmation that this interpretation is correct, look at the other "he who overcomes" passages in Revelation chapters 2 and 3 and apply the same interpretation to them.

•Confusion because a Word Has Multiple Meanings

> *John 15:1-2, 6 I am the true vine, and My Father is the vinedresser. Every branch in Me that does not bear fruit, He takes away; and every that bears fruit, He prunes it, that it may bear more fruit. ... (verse 6) If*

anyone does not abide in Me, he is thrown away as a branch, and dries up; and they gather them, and cast them into the fire, and they are burned.

The analogy divides the human race into three categories of people: 1) branches in Him that are not bearing fruit, which get "taken away," 2) branches in Him that are bearing fruit, that get pruned, and 3) "anyone" who does not abide, who is thrown away as a branch. The question is about this phrase "He takes away." Fruitless believers, whom the Vinedresser "takes away". We have here a question of interpretation: which meaning of the Greek word *airo* best fits the context? *Airo* can mean "take away" (Matthew 13:12, John 1:29) but it can also means "raise," "lift up," or "pick up," as the lame man was told to "pick up" his pallet (John 5:8-12), seven baskets of fragments were "picked up" after multiplying the loaves (Matthew 15:37), we are told to "take up" our cross (Matthew 16:24) and follow. If it means "take away" it means something very different than "lift up."

Can the context help us? Within the context of the vineyard, at times a branch falls on the ground and gets covered with dust, and fails to bear fruit because it's not getting much sunlight. So the vinedresser picks it up off the ground, washes it off, and ties it up into the support structure so it can become productive again. I suggest that the context here gives us the meaning that the fruitless believer will not be "taken away" but "picked up" and placed back into service by the heavenly Vinedresser.

•Not Rightly Distinguishing between Heaven and Reward in Heaven

Some very serious warnings are given about losing reward in heaven and we can easily misunderstand these as warnings about losing heaven itself. We need to distinguish between the gift of eternal life and reward, which is earned.

> *1 Corinthians 9:27b ...lest possibly, after I have preached to others, I myself should be disqualified (Gr.: unapproved, unworthy).*

The word "disqualified" makes it sound as if Paul is fearful of losing his salvation! But taken in context, we see that the passage is an allusion to the Olympic games and the victors' wreaths. Let's go back two verses to verse 25, "And everyone who competes in the games exercises self-control in all things. They then do it to receive a perishable wreath, but we an imperishable. Therefore I run in such a way, as not without aim." Paul was not concerned about losing his salvation (he is the same man who wrote Romans 8:38-39, etc.) but about losing his reward in heaven, an imperishable victor's crown.

> *Hebrews 6:4-6 For in the case of those who have once been enlightened and have tasted of the heavenly gift and have been made partakers of the Holy Spirit, and have tasted the good word of God and the powers of the age to come, and then have fallen away, it is impossible to renew them again to repentance, since they again crucify to themselves the Son of God, and put Him to open shame. For ground that drinks the rain that falls upon it and brings forth vegetation useful to those for whose sake it is also tilled, receives a blessing from God; but if it yields thorns and thistles, it is worthless and close to being cursed, and it ends up being burned.*

Are the people discussed here true believers? Some try to dodge the implications by saying they are not, but I have to conclude that they are because they "have been enlightened" and "have tasted of the heavenly gift." They are also Spirit-baptized ("partakers of the Holy Spirit") and have experienced God's miracle power. (Some of us may not have experienced enough in our journey with the Lord for this scripture to even apply to us!) But then, these experienced Christians fell away and put Jesus to open shame, and are compared to ground that yields thorns & thistles after receiving God's rain. Let's examine three key phrases:

--"It ends up being burned."   This phrase makes some conclude that the people go to hell, and it certainly sounds that way upon first reading it. But does burning always mean hell? No. In chapter eleven we looked at 1 Corinthians 3:10-15, which speaks of a burning that tests our works at the judgment of rewards, and even addresses the case of some who will lose all reward but "shall be saved, yet so as through fire" (1 Corinthians 3:15). The fact that the thorns and thistles are burned does not prove that the people were lost.

-- "Close to being cursed." Here's a curious expression. Why does it say "close to" instead of just "cursed"? I think it's a crucial distinction. Anyone who goes to hell is cursed according to Matthew 25:41, "Depart from Me, accursed ones, into the eternal fire." But a Christian can't be cursed because Galatians 3:13 says, "Christ redeemed us from the curse of the Law, having become a curse for us." So the people described in Hebrews 6 come close to being cursed but can't be cursed because Jesus took the curse for them. They don't go to hell, but they come as close as possible to it without it happening.

-- "It is impossible to renew them again to repentance." They get into a condition from which they cannot repent. They have crossed a line from which it is impossible to come back, as Israel demonstrated after the tenth time of complaining in the wilderness (see Numbers 14). When the people of Israel complained and doubted God's care for the tenth time in spite of seeing His miraculous works among them, God determined they would not go into the Promised Land. Their children would, but they wouldn't. He didn't divorce them; He didn't stop providing for them; they were still His people, but there was no longer a way of repentance open to them to get back to His original plan of entering the Promised Land and receiving all that God had intended for them in this life. They had sinned a "sin unto death" (1 John 5:16), i.e. physical death. We don't know when a person has crossed the line. Hebrews 6 is a solemn warning to us not to remain in a condition of consistent disobedience or frustrate God's work in our lives, but it's not a warning that God will send a Christian to hell.

Even an early death caused by a "sin unto death" is evidence of God's mercy. When a person has hardened himself into a state of consistent disobedience, why should God leave him on earth any longer? A longer life will not give him time to repent, because he has passed that point. For him a longer life means more sin, and more sin means more judgment waiting. So in His mercy God takes the hardened Christian home early, before more time has passed to accumulate more sins for which he would have to answer. Even in judgment God remembers mercy (Habakkuk 3:2).

Years ago a young man named Tim began to attend our church, who had been saved out of a heroin addiction. After a short time he went back into drugs, but our pastor found him and brought him out. Another couple years went by, and Tim again backslid, went home to New York City and once more became involved with his addiction. Pastor Tom pursued him to New York and brought him out again, but this time the Lord impressed on the pastor to tell the young man that if he backslid another time the Lord would take him home (he would die). Praise the Lord that Tim did not backslide after that. The warning the pastor gave kept him from a "sin unto death."

What More Can God Say?

An old hymn reads,

"How firm a foundation, you saints of the Lord,

Is laid for your faith in His excellent word!

What more can He say than to you He has said,

To you who for refuge to Jesus have fled?"

What more can He say? I mean, seriously? Maybe if He had said, "I'll never leave you" we would be more secure. (But wait, He did say that!) Well, maybe if He had said that no one was strong enough to take us away from Him. (Oops, He said that, too.) If He had said that we wouldn't even be judged, that would help. Or that nothing can separate us from His love.

You get the point: He said all these! But seriously, what other promise could He give that would put it to rest for you once and for all? What more can He say?

Our foundation is firm. Let these truths sink into your heart: Jesus is our Keeper; we can know we have eternal life; we have passed from judgment into life; the gift of salvation is irrevocable. Hopefully you are convinced that your salvation is secure, and can doubt no longer.

Chapter Sixteen
The New Covenant

Jeremiah 31:31-34 "Behold, days are coming," declares the Lord, "when I will make a new covenant with the house of Israel and with the house of Judah, not like the covenant which I made with their fathers in the day I took them by the hand to bring them out of the land of Egypt, My covenant which they broke, although I was a husband to them," declares the Lord. "But this is the covenant which I will make with the house of Israel after those days," declares the Lord, "I will put My law within them, and on their heart I will write it; and I will be their God, and they shall be My people. And they shall not teach again, each man his neighbor and each man his brother, saying, 'Know the Lord,' for they shall all know Me, from the least of them to the greatest of them," declares the Lord, "for I will forgive their iniquity, and their sin I will remember no more."

What's the difference between the New Testament, or New Covenant ["testament" and "covenant" are translations of the same word] and the Old? Few scriptures compare them as explicitly as this one. Jeremiah prophesied hundreds of years before Jesus came and gave us details of the change Jesus would bring to our relationship with God. If we explore the fuller meanings of the Greek words for "new" and "covenant" (used when Jeremiah's words are quoted in the New Testament), we'll see how great a change it is, so great that Hebrews 8:13 declares, "When He said, 'A new covenant,' He has made the first obsolete."

"Covenant"

Greek has two choices of words for covenant or contract. The first is a *suntheke*, a bilateral contract. An example of a bilateral contract is a business contract, for instance, a workman repairs your house and you pay him money. If he doesn't do the repairs he has broken his part of the agreement and if you don't pay the money you've broken your part. Another example is a marriage: the bride says "I do" and the groom says "I do," and each one is responsible to uphold their vow.

The Old Covenant was bilateral, an agreement between God and the people, therefore each had their part to uphold.

> *Exodus 24:7-8 Then he took the Book of the Covenant and read it in the hearing of the people; and they said, "All that the Lord has spoken we will do, and we will be obedient!" So Moses took the blood and sprinkled it on the people, and said, "Behold, the blood of the covenant, which the Lord has made with you in accordance with all these words."*

God said: Do this and you will live; you keep the commandments, and I will bless you. The people said: We will do it! How little they knew about human nature! "My covenant which they broke," is God's commentary in Exodus 24:32.

The second Greek word for contract is *diatheke*, a unilateral contract. A unilateral covenant depends on one party only. An example is a will. When a will is read and grandfather's words are, "I leave to my Grandson Jeff my house at 105 Oak Drive," the fulfillment of that depends only on what Grandfather wanted. It will happen without the grandson "earning" it or doing anything except signing the ownership deed. Grandson Jeff can refuse to accept the gift, but he can't do anything to stop it being offered. This is how it is with the new covenant; it is a *diatheke*, a one-sided agreement, based on a promise from one to another.

In our system of law, there are four parts to a gift. The giver must 1) have the will to give, 2) have the ability to give, 3) actually present the gift, and then 4) the gift must be received. If all four of these happen, it is a gift according to the law. Our part in the new covenant is number four, to receive. Our choice is whether to receive this gift of salvation offered to us by God, or refuse to receive. The new covenant is based not on obeying or disobeying, but on receiving or not receiving.

We've seen that Moses' covenant was bilateral. What about the covenant God made with Abraham, which predates Moses' covenant by 400 years? Was it bilateral or unilateral? This holds significance for us, because the letter to the Galatians tells us that the "new covenant" is a continuation of and actually started with God's covenant with Abraham.

> *Galatians 3:16-19 Now the promises were spoken to Abraham and to his seed. He does not say, "And to your seeds," as to many, but to one, "And to your seed," that is, Christ. What I am saying is this: the Law, which came four hundred and thirty years later, does not invalidate a covenant previously ratified by God, so as to nullify the promise. For if the inheritance is based on law, it is no longer based on a promise. But God has granted it to Abraham by means of a promise. Why the Law, then? It was added because of transgressions, having been ordained through angels by the agency of a mediator, until the Seed should come to whom the promise had been made.*

To answer our question about Abraham's covenant being bilateral or unilateral, let's look at something that happened between Abraham and God in Genesis 15.

> *Genesis 15:7-10, 17-18. And He said to him, "I am the Lord who brought you out of Ur of the Chaldeans, to give you*

> *this land to possess it." And he said, "O Lord God, how may I know that I shall possess it?" So He said to him, "Bring Me a three-year-old heifer, and a three-year-old female goat, and a three-year-old ram, and a turtledove, and a young pigeon." Then he brought all these to Him and cut them in two, and laid each half opposite the other; but he did not cut the birds...(verse 17) And it came about when the sun had set, that it was very dark, and behold, a smoking oven and a flaming torch which passed between these pieces. On that day the Lord made a covenant with Abram, saying, "To your descendants I have given this land..."*

When Abram asked for extra assurance from God and God told him to bring some animals, Abram knew exactly what God had in mind. He and God were about to "cut the covenant." The ancient custom for two people making a contract was to kill an animal, cut it in two, and walk together between the pieces. By these actions they were vowing, "May I be killed and cut in two, if I don't keep my part of our agreement." Abram fully expected that he and God would walk together between the pieces of the animals, each pledging to do their part in keeping the agreement. Abraham would continue to walk with God and obey His commands, and God would deliver the land to him. But then something very unusual happened – Abram did not walk between the pieces! Instead, a deep sleep came on him and he saw representations of the Father and the Holy Spirit pass between the pieces - the Father came to consume and the Holy Spirit to examine the sacrifice of the Son. But did Abraham walk through? No! The absence of Abraham changed the covenant from bilateral to unilateral: God took all the responsibility to fulfill His promise, and Abraham would be given the land unequivocally, regardless of his future behavior.

"New"

The Greek language also has two words for "new," *neos* and *kainos*. *Neos* means "new in time," like a new Toyota – newly made at the factory. *Kainos* means "new in quality," like a new type of car, a model of car not invented before. A new bottle of Coke is a *neos* bottle of Coke. But to describe a newly invented and different type of Coke (for instance the unpopular "new Coke" when it was introduced), *kainos* would be used. One is new in time, the other new in quality.

The New Covenant is *kainos* (Hebrews 8:8f) -- new & different, new and "not-like." It is "not like," Jeremiah tells us, by being internal,

Old Covenant	New Covenant
Didn't change human nature, just sought to limit certain behaviors which aggravated the problem (Rom. 7:8 *"But sin, taking opportunity through the commandment, produced in me coveting of every kind..."*)	Transforms human nature. (Rom. 8:2 "For the law of the Spirit of life in Christ Jesus has set you free from the law of sin and death.")
Tried to change people from the **external**.	Starts inside and works out... **Internal**.

inclusive, and effective.

The new and not-like covenant is **internal**, written upon hearts instead of stone: (v.33) "I will put My law within them, and on their heart I will write it."

The Old Covenant didn't change human nature, it just sought to limit certain behaviors, and the prohibitions actually aggravated the problem: Romans 7:8 "But sin, taking opportunity thru the commandment, produced in me coveting of every kind." After being told not to covet, he found that coveting sprang up within him more than ever before. If you tell your child, "You can do anything except touch the TV screen. It can fall on you or you can break it, it's dangerous," you know what happens next! The TV suddenly becomes the most enticing thing in the world and your child has to touch it. Don't you react this way to a "Keep Off The Grass" sign? The rule is a good rule, there's nothing wrong it, but something is wrong with us, and this good rule has now highlighted the perverseness in human nature which wasn't seen clearly until the rule was put in effect.

In contrast, the New Covenant provides for human nature to be transformed:

Romans 8:2 "For the law of the Spirit of life in Christ Jesus has set you free from the law of sin and of death."

We now have a new law operating in the Christian, which frees him from the law of sin. Think of the law of gravity as representing the "law of sin and death." Gravity seems inescapable, until one day we discover a law that can overcome it, called the law of aerodynamics. If you make wings in a certain shape and move forward fast enough, the air passing across the wings will cause a vacuum into which the plane will rise, overpowering the law of gravity. (I'm always amazed to be up close to a 747 and realize that it can actually rise from the ground!) In the same way the "law of the Spirit of life in Christ Jesus" makes us rise above the "law of sin and death."

The Old Covenant was external, the New internal. The Old Covenant tried to change people from outside; by placing external restrictions on people it attempted to change them on the inside. It was primarily concerned with externals, not with what was happening in a person's heart. In contrast, the New Covenant starts inside a person and works toward the outside behavior. Jesus talked a lot about what is happening in our hearts. If our heart is correct, then the external behaviors will become so, also.

The new & not-like covenant is **inclusive**: (v.34) "they shall all know Me."

It is not just for one nation, but open to all. What a lovely word, "all." We can come regardless of birth, wealth, or position. The Old had class distinctions by birth. Only descendants of Levi could serve in the temple, and selected from them, only descendants of Aaron could serve as priests and enter the temple itself, then from the priests only the High Priest could enter the Holy of Holies. These people were chosen to serve in these positions not by gift, talent, or desire, but only because of the family into which they were born. Access to God was restricted based on a person's birth.

In the New, access to God embraces all. Everyone who enters into the new covenant has a real experience of God. Listen to these comments on the Transfiguration from Watchman Nee:

> "There was Moses standing for the law, and there was Elijah for the prophets, and, in proposing to prolong the mountain-top experience, Peter would make provision for these two alongside the Lord. ...
>
> God's word made it clear that now, with the coming of the Kingdom, these were to give way before it. 'The law and the prophets were until John: from that time the gospel of the kingdom of God is preached' (Luke 16:16). ...The law and prophets must yield to the Kingdom of Jesus Christ; they cannot claim equal place with it. ...
>
> The law is the written word which expresses the will of God; the prophets are the living men who also express that will. In Old Testament days God usually expressed His will to ordinary Israelites by one or other of these means. For God dwelt not in man's heart but in an unapproachable Holy of holies. How then could man inquire of Him? First he could do so by reference to the law. Suppose he desired to know the appropriate procedure for dealing with

leprosy or defilement with a dead body, or whether or not he might use a particular species of animal or bird for food, he would go with his question to the Book of the law. By careful searching he would find the answer there, and he might do so without direct personal reference to God Himself. But suppose instead he wished to know whether or not he should go on a particular journey to a particular place. What would he do then? He would turn to a prophet and say, 'Kindly inquire of the Lord for me whether I should make this journey or not.' But here again the answer came to him second-hand, as it were. He had no authority to go to God direct. Whether through law or prophets, his knowledge of God always came to him indirectly, through a book or through a man; never by direct revelation from God Himself.

But that is not Christianity. Christianity always involves a personal knowledge of God through His Spirit, and not merely the knowing of His will through the medium of a man or a book. Many Christians today have a book knowledge of Christ; they know Him indeed through God's own Book, but they have no vital relationship with Him. Worse still, many know Him only 'by hearsay', from their pastor or from some other man, but they are not in direct communication with Him. Their knowledge is outward, not inward; and let me affirm that anything short of a personal, inward revelation of the Lord is not Christianity. In seeking to know God's will under the old covenant, men were restricted to the law and the prophets, but under the New Covenant God has promised that 'they shall not teach each his fellow-citizen, and each his brother, saying, Know the Lord; because all shall know me in themselves, from the little one unto the great among them' (Hebrews 8:11; J.N. Darby New Translation). 'You shall know Him in yourselves.' Christianity is based not on information but on revelation. That is where the Lord began with Peter: 'Blessed are you, Simon,...for flesh and blood has not revealed this to you, but my Father which is in heaven.' The Kingdom of God is founded on a personal knowledge of the Lord which comes through a direct speaking by Him and a direct hearing by you and me. ...

That was the lesson Peter had to learn. In the Kingdom there is only one Voice to be heard, through whatever medium it speaks. I still have the written Scriptures and I still have my brother's 'prophetic' word (for Moses and Elijah were there on the mount!). Christianity is not independent of men and books -- far from it. But the way of the Kingdom is that the 'beloved Son' speaks directly to me personally and directly, and that personally and directly I hear Him." (Watchman Nee, *What Shall This Man Do?*, CLC 1973, pp.20-24.)

The new & not-like covenant is **effective**: (v.34) "for I will forgive their iniquity, and their sin I will remember no more." The sin problem is really dealt with; forgiveness & reconciliation are attained, and a clear conscience is the result. The Old Testament uses the word "atonement" (to "cover over" sin) 75 times, but in the New Testament "atonement" is practically unused (only once). Instead of "atonement", we have "redemption" from sin. In the Old Testament sin was covered over but still there; in the New Testament sin is removed! How?

> Hebrews 9:12 "not through the blood of goats & calves, but through His own blood, He entered the holy place once for all, having obtained eternal redemption."

We are redeemed! Jesus' blood is so much more effective than the blood of goats and calves! Our sin is not just covered over, it is removed -- forgiven and forgotten! On papyrus scrolls, if they rinsed a page with water, the ink would totally dissolve and run off the page with the water. That is what happened to the record of our sins when we received Jesus as our Savior!

In conclusion, then, let's see how the letter to the Hebrews sums up the benefits of this new covenant with God.

> *Hebrews 10:19-22 Since therefore, brethren, we have confidence to enter the holy place by the blood of Jesus, by a new and living way which He inaugurated for us through the veil, that is, His flesh, and since we have a great priest over the house of God, let us draw near with a sincere heart in full assurance of faith...*

We have confidence to enter God's presence because of the blood of Jesus; we have a new way through the veil; we have a great priest; what more could we ask? Let us draw near in full assurance!

Appendix A

Is Water Baptism Essential for Salvation (Justification)?

We touched on this, but let's examine two scriptures that are misinterpreted by some. The first is in Jesus' interview with Nicodemus: John 3:5 "Truly, truly, I say to you, unless one is born of water and the Spirit, he cannot enter the kingdom of God."

Some teach that "born of water" means water baptism, saying that unless one is baptized and born of the Spirit, he cannot be saved. By looking at the verse in its context we understand that "born of water" refers to natural birth (born out of the amniotic fluid), not water baptism.

> *John 3:3-5 Jesus answered and said to him, "Truly, truly, I say to you, unless one is born again, he cannot see the kingdom of God." Nicodemus said to Him, "How can a man be born when he is old? He cannot enter a second time into his mother's womb and be born, can he? Jesus answered, "Truly, truly, I say to you, unless one is born of water and the Spirit, he cannot enter into the kingdom of God. That which is born of the flesh is flesh, and that which is born of the Spirit is spirit."*

Nicodemus' question in verse 4 shows that he interprets "born again" to mean a second physical birth; he is thinking only of the physical realm. Jesus answers him that one must be "born of water" (born physically) "and the Spirit" (born spiritually). Rephrasing the same thought in verse 6, Jesus talks about "that which is born of the flesh" (physical birth) and "that which is born of the Spirit" (spiritual birth). This type of parallel construction, which Jesus uses in verses 5 and 6, is common to Hebrew thought and poetry. Those who interpret "born of water" as water baptism have wrenched this phrase totally out of the context of the discussion.

A second scripture that is used to teach that baptism is necessary for salvation is

> *Mark 16:16 He who has believed and has been baptized shall be saved; but he who has disbelieved shall be condemned.*

Based on this, some say, "You see, if you believe and are baptized you will be saved." If you believe and are baptized you will be saved, that's true. But is this verse saying water baptism is a requirement for salvation? We should recognize that there are four possibilities:

The cases addressed by Mark 16:16 are number 1 (believing and baptized) and numbers 3 and 4 (disbelieving, no matter what the person does concerning baptism). But does this scripture address #2, the case of someone who believes but is not baptized? It does not -- maybe because it should be a rare occurrence, an anomaly. So we ask ourselves if we have any example of someone in category 2, who believed in Jesus but for some reason was not baptized? Yes! You may have already thought of one of the thieves who died beside Jesus on a cross, to whom Jesus promised fellowship with Him in Paradise!

To make Mark 16:16 say that without baptism we won't be

One Believe Baptized	Two Believe Not Baptized
Three Not Believe Baptized	Four Not Believe Not Baptized

saved is forcing the verse to say what it does not say.

Appendix B
Schools of Thought concerning the Millennium

There are 3 schools of thought concerning the millennium. Are you amillennial, premillennial, or postmillennial? (This is not talking about when Jesus comes back in relation to the rapture, but when Jesus comes back in relation to the millennium.)

Premillennial thinking holds that Revelation 20 and other passages are to be interpreted literally and refer to a literal, physical return of Jesus Christ before ("pre") the start of the millennium. In this view, it is Jesus' own personal presence that brings about the defeat of the Anti-Christ and inaugurates Jesus' rule over the nations and the thousand-year peace.

Amillennialism (the prefix "a" = "without") interprets Revelation 20 as symbolic rather than literal, spiritualizing any promise of the kingdom being restored to Israel or God ruling from Zion, etc. The only "reign" of Christ is that available to the Church, now in this age, according to those who do not believe in a millennium. Promises to Israel and Zion are seen as promises for the Church. "Liberal theology takes this viewpoint because of its objection to the miraculous character of predictive prophesy and its reductionistic approach to biblical inspiration." (Int'l Standard Bible Encyclopedia, vol.3 p.360, Eerdman's 1986.)

Postmillennialists think that Jesus will come back after ("post") the millennium, at the Day of Judgment. So if Jesus comes back after the thousand years, what causes His reign to begin? It is inaugurated by the Church as it becomes stronger and stronger, takes over the institutions of the world (governmental, educational, etc.), and brings in a reign of Christ on the earth. Postmillennialists believe it is the duty of the

Church to rise up and take over the institutions of the world and force a reign of righteousness upon the non-believing world. This interpretation was popular around 1700 but the history of the world since then discredited it for most people. Recently, however, postmillennialism has had a surprising resurgence. As you can imagine, if someone adopts this interpretation, it very significantly impacts the person's world-view and motivation.

Appendix C
Thoughts about the Unforgivable Sin

"What if I have committed the unforgivable sin?" Many believers carry this nagging question; when I have asked audiences for a show of hands if they are troubled by this, consistently one-third raise their hands. People may not know what it is, but they fear they have done it. Obviously, one-third of all Christians can't have committed the unpardonable sin; these doubts are evidently the work of the "accuser of the brethren" (Revelation 12:10).

The story goes that a dear old lady always had such kind things to say about people that it drove her more-critical friend to exasperation. He finally said, "I'll bet you even have something good to say about the Devil!" She thought a moment before replying, "Well, he's always on the job!"

The Devil is always on the job, and a big part of that job is being "the accuser of the brethren." "Devil" is a title and "Satan" a name, but neither is translated, just transliterated. If we translate them, "Devil" means "Divider," and "Satan" means "Accuser" or "Adversary."

The Accuser's accusations run in at least four directions: accusing us to God, accusing us to each other, accusing us to ourselves, and accusing God to us. We see him busy at his work in Job chapter one, where he accuses Job to God: 'Of course he loves you, God – look how You've blessed him! But if You remove your blessings, he will curse You!' This sets up the whole trial of the book of Job.

You've heard his accusations inside your head: 'You idiot, look what you just did!' 'If people at church knew what you just thought!!' We've all heard similar thoughts. Maybe we imagined we were talking to ourselves, or even that God was talking to us this way, but all thoughts like these are not from God but from the devil. Recognize that the devil's thoughts originate from him and not from you and that he is responsible for their content; therefore, they reflect on his character, not yours. In my experience, the whisperings of the Accuser account for the vast majority of the worries Christians have about the unpardonable sin. "Submit therefore to God. Resist the devil and he will flee from you" (James 4:7).

I have two questions for us to consider: 1) What is the unforgivable sin? and 2) Will one unforgiven sin keep a person out of heaven?

1) Jesus identified the unforgivable sin as blasphemy against the Holy Spirit.

> Mark 3:22, 28-30 *And the scribes who came down from Jerusalem were saying, "He is possessed by Beelzebul," and "He casts out the demons by the ruler of the demons." ... (verse 28) Truly I say to you, all sins shall be forgiven the sons of men, and whatever blasphemies they utter; but whoever blasphemes against the Holy Spirit never has forgiveness, but is guilty of an eternal sin" – because they were saying, "He has an unclean spirit."*

From the context it seems that blasphemy (mocking or contemptuous speech) against the Holy Spirit means attributing to the devil the work of the Holy Spirit. The scribes witnessed the miracles Jesus did through the Holy Spirit, but said it was the devil working. They said this not because they thought that was the truth, but because they saw Jesus as a threat to their positions of influence. Unless you have seen the work of the Holy Spirit and knowingly attributed it to the devil, you haven't committed this sin.

2) But what if you have done this sin? Is your case hopeless?

Since it is an "eternal sin" it cannot be forgiven, but I have hope even in this case: although it can't be forgiven, it can be cleansed. Hebrews 9:22 "And according to the Law, almost all things are cleansed with blood..." It says "almost" because a few things in the Old Testament were not cleansed by sprinkling blood on them, but by passing them through a fire (see Numbers 31:22-23). This remedy would apply to blasphemy against the Spirit by a Christian (if it's even possible), and also to other sins for which Christians have not repented. All unrepentant areas will pass through the fire, and the fire will do its cleansing so that they can enter heaven (1 Corinthians 3:10-15).

Appendix D
Calvinism & Arminianism

I realize that this topic is too technical to keep the interest of most readers, but I offer it as my contribution to anyone who has struggled with making sense of one or the other of these approaches. I also offer it to make clear to some who would write me off as "a Calvinist" that I am not comfortable with that label. I find that I am not comfortable in either camp, and think the truth lies between the two but mostly with Arminius. I also include it because although these issues are seldom faced directly in our day, the schools of thought still have influence in our clergy and denominations.

The 1600s witnessed the development of two systems of thinking about salvation. One emphasized the sovereignty of God and the other emphasized the free will of man. The first was based on the work of Protestant reformer John [Jean] Calvin (1509-1564), the second on a response to Calvin by Dutch theologian James Arminius (1560-1609). These doctrines are not based on revelation from God alone (the Bible), but on a combination of revelation and the logic of the Enlightenment, or logic applied to the revelation God has given. Theologians have debated over the last 400 years without being able to finally resolve the differences, and in the end we may have to conclude that some of what we are studying is a mystery which we cannot fully comprehend. In fact, in Institutes of the Christian Religion (Book 3, ch.21, section 1) Calvin himself warned against looking too deeply in to the subject -- but it didn't stop his followers from doing just that! But we should be aware of the two approaches, and realize that we all hold certain beliefs that fall into one system or the other. And if we will stand on the shoulders of these giants who have gone before us, and take advantage of the advances in scholarship available to us that they did not have, maybe we'll be able to see further than they did! We'll look first at the teaching of each system, then compare these with scripture and each other.

The Five Points of Calvinism

Calvinism, also called "Reformed theology," is based on John Calvin's Institutes of the Christian Religion, first published in 1536. Calvinism has a rich history: Scotch Presbyterians, French Huguenots, English Puritans, American Pilgrims and present-day Baptist, Presbyterian, and Reformed churches trace their roots to Calvin (although how closely they follow his teaching varies). The starting point for Calvin was the sovereignty of God: God rules over all and overrules; God does whatever He pleases. Calvin reasoned that if God is in control of everything, then He is also in control of who will become saved and who will not, and to say less takes away from His position as God of the universe, and thus makes salvation dependent to some extent on works instead of grace. Fifty-five years after his death, , the leadership of the Dutch Reformed Church called a Council of church leaders (note: many "Reformed Theology" leaders from other like-minded groups attended) that became known as the Synod of Dort, which should not be confused with Councils of the entire Christian Church. This council then drafted The Canons of the Synod of Dort (1619), in which they set out the "five points of Calvinism" which are summarized below.

1) Total Depravity. Man is totally unable to save himself. Man's spirit is dead in trespasses and sins, his will is corrupted because he has inherited the sin nature from Adam (called "original sin"), and he is incapable of choosing to be saved.

John 6:44 No one can come to Me, unless the Father who sent Me draws him...

> *Ephesians 2:3 we too all formerly...were by nature children of wrath*
>
> *Romans 5:16 The judgment followed one sin and brought condemnation.*

2) Unconditional Election. Before the world was created, God chose ("elected") some people to be saved. His choice was irrespective of their desire to be saved (because no-one has that desire apart from God working in him), and was not according to anything the person did or would do, but was totally dependent on God's will alone. (The strictest Calvinists include a "double election," meaning that some are also chosen to go to hell. Calvin himself taught double election but the Synod of Dort did not.)

> *Ephesians 1:4-5 He chose us in Him before the foundation of the world, that we should be holy and blameless before Him. In love He predestined us to adoption as sons through Jesus Christ to Himself, according to the kind intention of His will.*
>
> *1 Peter 2:8 They stumble because they are disobedient to the word, and to this they were also appointed.*
>
> *Romans 9:16 So then it does not depend on the man who runs or the man who wills, but on God who has mercy.*

3) Limited Atonement. Because God's grace is "efficient" (that God would not punish Christ for sins and later punish a person for those same sins, the payment having been made), Christ died only for the sins of the elect, not for the sins of the entire world. Scriptures that say that Christ died for his people are used as support. (Some Calvinists do not believe in limited atonement.)

> *John 10:11 I am the good shepherd, the good shepherd lays down his life for the sheep.*

4) Irresistible Grace. Those who have been chosen by God for salvation will be drawn to respond to the gospel, in spite of their resistance to God or desire not to be saved.

> *John 6:37 All that the Father gives Me shall come to Me.*
>
> *Acts 13:48 When the Gentiles heard this, they were glad and honored the word of the Lord; and all who were appointed for eternal life believed.*

5) Perseverance of the Saints. Also called "eternal security." A person who has truly been born again cannot lose or undo his salvation. All the chosen will spend eternity in heaven. Not only our initial salvation but also keeping our salvation depends on God, not on man.

> *1 Peter 1:23, 25 For you have been born again not of seed which is perishable but imperishable, through the living and abiding word of God... 'the word of the Lord abides forever.' And this is the word which was preached to you.*
>
> *John 10:28 I give eternal life to them, and they shall never perish; no one can snatch them out of my hand.*

Negative fruit of Calvinism can include:

Diminished motivation for evangelism. If God has already chosen those who will be saved, and they will be saved regardless of what happens, why work to spread the gospel, give money to evangelistic works, or go to foreign mission fields? What we do will not change the outcome! The Calvinist would respond that he evangelizes to see God call forth those who will respond to the preaching of the gospel, and that his doctrine encourages him to work even where he sees no results because he knows God has chosen some for salvation who will irresistibly come.

Haughtiness and a class distinction. The attitude of the Pharisees that they were the true sons of Abraham while the multitude was "accursed" could find a successor in Calvin's teaching: we are the elect and they are not. It would hold that some are impossible to save, beyond God's grace because not of His choosing.

Despair of being saved by tender-hearted seekers, who doubt that God has chosen them.

Permission to sin. 'Why not live in sin, if I'm going to heaven no matter what?' Charles Spurgeon, famous preacher of the 1800s, wrote, "It is to be feared that Calvinistic doctrine becomes most evil teaching when it is set forth by men of ungodly lives, and exhibited as if it were a cloak for licentiousness..." (C.H. Spurgeon, *Lectures to My Students*, Zondervan 1969 p.8.)

Arminianism

James Arminius began as a strict Calvinist, but later objected to the Reformed system, especially to the thought of a limited atonement. His teachings were published one year after his death in The Remonstrance (1610) and are the basis for Methodist, Nazarene, Free Will Baptist, Pentecostal, and many charismatic churches today. The starting point for Arminius was the free will of man: that God offers salvation for "whosoever will," and that God gives all people the ability to respond to the gospel. A summary of Arminianism follows.

A) Prevenient Grace. In this first point, Calvinism and Arminianism are in general agreement that mankind is totally unable to make a move toward God or salvation. Arminius taught "prevenient grace," that the Holy Spirit works with a person previous to conversion to enable him to respond to the gospel. (A minor point of dispute under this heading is whether original sin by itself is enough to condemn a person, or whether each one has to sin individually. Calvin said man is condemned as a result of Adam's fall while Arminius said people have to sin individually to be condemned.)

John 12:32 And I, if I be lifted up from the earth, will draw all men to Myself.

John 16:8 And He, when He comes, will convict the world concerning sin, and righteousness, and judgment.

B) Conditional Election. Before the world began, God chose those who would be saved based on His foreknowledge that they would respond to the gospel. God does not choose anyone for hell; each person is responsible for his own destiny by his own acceptance or rejection of the work of Christ on his behalf. Arminians do not consider faith to be a work, since faith merely receives the gift of salvation. (If someone holds out a gift of money to you and you reach out to take it, did you just "work" for it by reaching out? Romans 4:5 supports Arminians' interpretation that faith is not a work by contrasting faith and works, putting them in different categories.)

1 Peter 1:1-2 who are chosen according to the foreknowledge of God the Father, by the sanctifying work of the Spirit, that you may obey Jesus Christ and be sprinkled with His blood

Romans 8:29 For whom He foreknew, He also predestined to become conformed to the image of His Son, that He might be the first-born among many brethren.

Romans 4:5 But to the one who does not work, but believes in Him who justifies the ungodly, his faith is reckoned as righteousness.

C) Unlimited Atonement. Christ died for the sins of the whole world, not only for the sins of the elect. Christ's redemption is therefore sufficient for all people, but effective only for those who believe. Every person is savable and no one is a hopeless case.

John 3:16 For God so loved the world, that He gave His only begotten Son, that whoever believes in Him should not perish, but have eternal life.

> *1 John 2:2 And He is the propitiation for our sins; and not for ours only, but for those of the whole world.*
>
> *2 Corinthians 5:9 God was in Christ reconciling the world to Himself, not counting their trespasses against them, and He has committed to us the word of reconciliation.*
>
> *1 Timothy 4:10 ...the living God, who is the Savior of all men, especially of believers.*

D) Resistible Grace. God draws all people toward Himself, but His offer of salvation can be refused. Humans are capable of resisting God's will.

> *1 Timothy 2:4 God our Savior, who desires all men to be saved and to come to the knowledge of the truth.*
>
> *Luke 7:30 But the Pharisees and lawyers rejected God's purpose for themselves.*
>
> *Matthew 23:37 O Jerusalem, Jerusalem, who kills the prophets and stones those who are sent to her! How often I wanted to gather your children together, the way a hen gathers her chicks under her wings, and you were unwilling.*
>
> *2 Peter 1:10 Therefore, brethren, be all the more diligent to make certain about His calling and choosing you; for as long as you do these things, you will never stumble.*

E) Conditional Perseverance. A person can choose to reject God and lose his salvation even after he has been born again. A person must abide in Christ to be saved, and can choose to walk away from the Lord. Arminius himself was undecided about this point [N] but later Arminians accepted it.

> *John 15:4, 6 Abide in Me, and I in you. As the branch cannot bear fruit of itself, unless it abides in the vine, so neither can you, unless you abide in Me. ... If anyone does not abide in Me, he is thrown away as a branch, and dries*

up; and they gather them, and cast them into the fire, and they are burned.

Negative fruit of Arminianism can include:

The need to be saved again and again. The wonder and joy of justification is overshadowed by a concern for good works to keep this salvation. Fearing that sin has caused people to lose their salvation, some churches continually call for their members to be saved again.

Doubts about God's love. Many sincere believers have lived in tormenting fear because they felt condemned each time they sinned, or when they felt emotionally distant from God, taking this as evidence that they were no longer saved.

Pride. If we share in the responsibility, shouldn't we share in the credit for our salvation? Historically, Arminianism led to the teaching of "sinless perfection" – that the Christian can attain a state of not sinning. This fosters an attitude of superiority when people feel they are doing well, or condemnation when falling short.

Delaying our own commitment to God, because the offer is so broad. Continuing Spurgeon's quote from above, he goes on, "...and Arminianism, on the other hand, with its wide sweep of the offer of mercy, may do most serious damage to the souls of men, if the careless tone of the preacher leads his hearers to believe that they can repent whenever they please; and that, therefore, no urgency surrounds the gospel message." (C.H. Spurgeon, *Lectures to My Students*, Zondervan 1969 p.8.)

A Few Scriptures as they are interpreted by Calvinists and Arminians

John 6:44 "No one can come to Me, unless the Father who sent Me draws him; and I will raise him up on the last day."

Calvinists (C): This teaches total depravity and unconditional election.

Arminians (A): Agree that it teaches total depravity. But they argue that through Jesus' death the Father draws all people: John 12:32 "And I, if I be lifted up from the earth, will draw all people unto Me."

John 15:16 "You did not choose Me, but I chose you, and appointed you, that you should go and bear fruit."

C: This supports unconditional election. Jesus did the choosing, not the person.

A: In context, the choosing referred to is not for salvation but for fruitfulness. Judas was "chosen" but not saved: John 6:70 "Did I Myself not choose you, the twelve, and yet one of you is a devil?"

Acts 13:48 "And when the Gentiles heard this, they began rejoicing and glorifying the word of the Lord; and as many as had been appointed to eternal life believed."

C: A proof text for unconditional election.

A: The verb *tetagmenoi* [had been appointed] is in the middle/passive voice, which leaves the meaning ambiguous. In Greek the same form is used for both the middle and the passive voices. If translated using the middle voice, the verse would read "as many as set themselves to eternal life believed"; if using the passive voice "as many as had been appointed to eternal life believed." A verse which can be legitimately translated either way should not be used as a proof text.

> Ephesians 1:4-5 *"just as He chose us in Him before the foundation of the world, that we should be holy and blameless before Him. In love He predestined us to adoption as sons through Jesus Christ to Himself, according to the kind intention of His will"*

C: This proves unconditional election, that before the world was made God made a choice about who would be saved and these were predestined to be adopted as sons.

A: Arminians maintain that:

"adoption as sons" does not refer to justification, but to glorification, as proved by Romans 8:23 "waiting eagerly for our adoption as sons, the redemption of our body." In other words, one thing God predetermined was that all who were justified by Christ would also be raised from the dead to live with Him. Romans 8:30 "whom He did predestine, them He also called; and whom He called, them He also justified; and whom He justified, them He also glorified."

The phrase "in Him" is key; that Christ was the chosen one (Isaiah 42:1); people become "in Him" through faith and thus become chosen along with Him.

The choosing is because of God's foreknowledge, i.e. that God saw the response the person would have. 1 Peter 1:1-2 "...chosen according to the foreknowledge of God the Father" and Romans 8:29 "For whom He foreknew, He also predestined..."

Conclusions

Calvinists and Arminians are in basic agreement about point 1.

Point three's "limited atonement" is clearly unscriptural (1 John 2:2; 1 Timothy 4:10) and Calvinists were wrong to change the biblical language of God's love for the world into "everlasting love for the elect" (Canons of the Synod of Dort, 2nd Head, Article 9). The position that Jesus died "for His people" (Matthew 1:21) is easily reconciled with Jesus dying for the sins of the whole world; if He died for all, it included His people. Many Calvinists join their voices with Arminius' objection to "limited atonement."

As to points 2 and 4, everyone agrees that God chose people, but the question becomes what this "choosing" means. Calvin maintains that God's choosing is not because of the person at all, but only because of God's sovereign will. Arminius posits that the choosing is caused by the prior knowledge God has, through which He sees the response people will have to His Son.

One strength of Arminius' position is that God's offer of salvation to "whoever will" remains a legitimate offer. All are savable and bear the responsibility for their own destiny. God does everything He can except violate people's wills and make the decision for them, including ordering when and where they were born (Acts 17:26-27), using circumstances in their lives, sending the Holy Spirit to "the world" (not just the elect) to convict of sin and judgment (John 16:8), putting the awareness of eternity in their hearts (Ecclesiastes 3:11); everything is done to convince them of their need for a Savior. If they don't respond, God is not to blame.

A weakness of Calvin's position is that God in this system of thought condemns people for not having a gift that only He can give but that He chose not to give! God alone possesses faith for salvation, and

He, in an "astonishing, mysterious, ineffable" [o] [inexpressible] way, deposits this gift in some but not all. God then examines each person to see if he has the gift or not. In my opinion, this is a distorted portrayal of God.

Calvinists see Ephesians 1:11 as a proof text for unconditional election. "That some receive the gift of faith from God, and others do not receive it, proceeds from God's eternal decree...'who works out everything in conformity with the purpose of his will' (Ephesians 1:11)" [p]. This presents God's will as being that some would be saved, and some lost, contradicting God is "not willing that any should perish, but that all should come to repentance." (2 Peter 3:9) If God's will can be resisted, so that "we do not yet see all things subjected to Him" (Hebrews 2:8), then what view do we take about the sovereignty of God, so important to Calvin's thought? Can God's sovereignty be limited without undermining His position as God? Certainly God can limit His own sovereignty without damaging His position. The Bible tells us that mankind's rebellion turned the dominion of this world over to the devil (2 Corinthians 4:4; Ephesians 2:2), but Jesus came to invade this present age with the authority of the age to come, with the result that His authority is already here for those who will voluntarily submit to it and will arrive one day for all of creation, when "every knee will bow" (Philippians 2:10). But until that day, God limits His sovereignty by respecting the sovereignty that He has placed within each person for his own life. He offers salvation but does not force it on anyone.

Another weakness in Calvin's system is that regeneration happens before anything else: regeneration enlightens the dark mind of the unbeliever, who then turns to the Lord. But according to 2 Corinthians 3:16, turning to the Lord comes before understanding, not vice versa: "but whenever a man turns to the Lord, the veil is taken away."

Lastly, how can a Calvinist explain 2 Peter 1:10, "Therefore, brethren, be all the more diligent to make certain about His calling and choosing you"? Under Calvinism, calling and election are totally God's work and will happen inexorably. What possible role can helpless men have in making certain about them?

This brings us to point five, eternal security, in which I find myself agreeing with Calvin's conclusion, but not because of the rest of his system of thought. What a person believes about the eternal security of the believer is so vital to our spiritual health and our concept of God that we will examine it in detail in the next two chapters.

For me, the final tally is Arminius 4 and Calvin 2: I find myself a four-point Arminian and a two-point Calvinist (because they agreed on point one, it doesn't add to five). Since Arminius himself leaned more toward the eternal security of the believer than not, maybe I'm as Arminian as Arminius! If you've read through all this, congratulations! I hope you've enjoyed our trek as we picked our way through this theological minefield.

Excerpts from the Canons of the Synod of Dort, 1619

Point 1, Total Depravity

"All men have sinned in Adam, lie under the curse, and are deserving of eternal death..." (1st Head, Art. 1).

"Unless the admirable Author of every good work so deal with us, man can have no hope of being able to rise from his fall by his own free will, by which, in a state of innocence, he plunged himself into ruin." (3rd & 4th Head, Art.16).

Point 2, Unconditional Election

"Election is the unchangeable purpose of God, whereby, before the foundation of the world, He has out of mere grace, according to the sovereign good pleasure of His own will, chosen from the whole human race...a certain number of persons to redemption in Christ...to bestow upon them true faith, justification, and sanctification, and... finally to glorify them. 'And those He predestined, he also called; those he called, he also justified; those he justified, he also glorified.' (Rom.8:30)" (1st Head, Art.7).

"This election was not founded upon foreseen faith and the obedience of faith, holiness, or any other good quality or disposition in man, as the prerequisite..." (1st Head, Art.9).

"That some receive the gift of faith from God, and others do not receive it, proceeds from God's eternal decree...'who works out everything in conformity with the purpose of his will' (Eph.1:11). According to which decree He graciously softens the hearts of the elect, however obstinate, and inclines them to believe; while He leaves the non-elect in His just judgment to their own wickedness and obduracy." (1st Head, Art.6).

"But that others who are called by the gospel obey the call and are converted is not to be ascribed to the proper exercise of free will... but it must be wholly ascribed to God." (3rd & 4th Head, Art.10).

Point 3, Limited Atonement

"The efficacy of the most precious death of His Son should extend to all the elect, for bestowing upon them alone the gift of justifying faith, thereby to bring them infallibly to salvation" (2nd Head, Art.8).

"This purpose, proceeding from everlasting love towards the elect..." (2nd Head, Art.9).

Point 4, Irresistible Grace

"...to bring them infallibly to salvation" (2nd Head, Art.8).

"The elect in due time...attain the assurance of this their eternal and unchangeable election." (1st Head, Art.12).

"It is evidently a supernatural work...astonishing, mysterious, and ineffable." (3rd & 4th Head, Art.12).

"Faith is therefore to be considered as the gift of God...because it is in reality conferred upon him, breathed and infused into him...because He who works in man both to will and to work...produces both the will to believe and the act of believing also." (3rd & 4th Head, Art.14).

"The Synod rejects the errors of those who teach that...man may resist God and the Holy Spirit, when God intends man's regeneration...and indeed man often does so resist that he prevents entirely his regeneration, and that it therefore remains in man's power to be regenerated or not. For this is nothing less than the denial of all that efficiency of God's grace in our conversion, and the subjecting of the working of Almighty God to the will of man, which is contrary to the apostles, who teach that we believe according to the working of the strength of his might (Eph.1:19); and that God fulfills every desire of goodness and every work of faith with power (2 Th.1:11); and that 'His divine power has given us everything we need for life and godliness' (2 Pe.1:3)." (3rd & 4th Head, Para.8)

Point 5, Perseverance of the Saints

"As God Himself is...unchangeable...and omnipotent, so the election made by Him can neither be interrupted nor changed, recalled, or annulled; neither can the elect by cast away; nor their number diminished." (1st Head, Art.11).

"Those who are converted could not persevere in that grace if left to their own strength. But God is faithful, who, having conferred grace, mercifully confirms and powerfully preserves them therein, even to the end." (5th Head, Art.3)

"The Synod rejects the errors of those who teach that...true believers and regenerate not only can fall from justifying faith...but indeed often do fall from this and are lost forever. ...for this...[is] contrary to the expressed words of the apostle Paul: 'Since we have now been justified by his blood, how much more shall we be saved from God's wrath through him (Rom.5:8-9).' ...and also contrary to the words of Jesus Christ: 'I give them eternal life, and they shall never perish; no one can snatch them out of my hand. My Father, who has given them to me, is greater than all; no one can snatch them out of my Father's hand' (John 10:28-29)." (5th Head, Para.3)

Endnotes, Appendix D

N "Though I here openly and ingenuously affirm, I never taught that *a true believer can either totally or finally fall away from the faith, and perish*; yet I will not conceal, that there are passages of Scripture which seem to me to wear this aspect; and those answers to them which I have been permitted to see, are not of such a kind as to approve themselves on all points to my understanding. On the other hand, certain passages are produced for the contrary doctrine [of unconditional perseverance] which are worthy of much consideration." (*The Writings of James Arminius*, vol.1, Baker 1956, p.254.)

O *Canons of the Synod of Dort*, 3rd & 4th Head, Article 12

P *Canons of the Synod of Dort*, 1st Head, Article 6. Instead, the predestination in Ephesians 1:11 refers not to the election of unbelievers to salvation but to believers being predestined to bring glory to God.

Appendix E
Predestined – to What?

Today "predestination" is an inflammatory term, so much so that we generally avoid using it altogether because it will just start an argument. Yet when Paul wrote his letters, it was a concept that made him rejoice. What are we missing that he saw?

The meaning of the Greek word *proorisas* ("to determine beforehand, to predestine") is not disputed. The dispute comes from the application of the word. Maybe we have become so focused on the word that we've missed its context. "The important thing for us to consider when the word is used is not who are the objects of this predestination, but what they are predestined to." (Spiros Zodhiates, *The Complete Word Study New Testament*, AMG 1991, p.938.) Let's consider the six times the word occurs.

In two references, the object of the predetermination is not individual justification but the overall plan of salvation. 1) 1 Corinthians 2:7 "But we speak God's wisdom in a mystery, the hidden wisdom, which God predestined before the ages to our glory." 2) Acts 4:27-28 "For truly in this city there were gathered together against thy holy servant Jesus, whom thou didst anoint, both Herod and Pontius Pilate, along with the Gentiles and the peoples of Israel, to do whatever thy hand and thy purpose predestined to occur."

A third reference addresses sanctification and glorification, but not justification. 3) Romans 8:29 "For whom He foreknew, He also did predestine to become conformed to the image of his Son, that He might be the first-born among many brethren." The object of the predestination is "to become conformed to the image of his Son." Maybe this is the beautiful truth we've missed: knowing beforehand all who would be saved, the Father made up his mind that anyone who did become saved would come to resemble Jesus in character, motives, and life, and one day would receive an imperishable body like Jesus' resurrected body. "In Rom.8:29 it is used with a personal object, the relative pronoun *hous* ['whom' in the plural]. This personal pronoun applies also to the previous verb, *proegno* [foreknew]. The purpose of this foreordination is expressed in the phrase, 'to be conformed to the image of His Son.'" (ibid.)

Next, we find one and only one reference that connects predestination and justification. It occurs in the very next verse after the one we just read. 4) Romans 8:30 "and whom He predestined, these He also called; and whom He called, these He also justified; and whom He justified, these He also glorified." "The occurrence in Romans 8:30 is to be explained by verse 29, in which it is clearly stated that this

1 Corinthians 2:7	
Acts 4:27	The plan of salvation was predetermined.
Romans 8:29	To resemble Jesus.
Romans 8:30	To be called, justified, & glorified – based on God's foreknowledge [of who would choose Jesus].
Ephesians 1:5	To be placed into our legal position as sons.
Ephesians 1:11	To bring God glory

foreordination was neither capricious nor an independent concept that was complete in itself. It was joined with the verb 'foreknew'." (ibid)

Another concept enters as we find we are predestined to "adoption as sons," i.e. being placed into a legal position of sonship – which will be experienced partially during this life, but fully when Jesus comes again. 5) Ephesians 1:5 "He predestined us to adoption as sons through Jesus Christ to Himself, according to the kind intention of His will." "In Ephesians 1:5 the purpose of the foreordination is the adoption, which means the placing of those who were born of God into their proper position (*huiothesia*, which is from *huios* [son] and the verb *tithemi* [to place])." (ibid)

The object of the last occurrence is bringing glory to God. 6) Ephesians 1:11 "We have obtained an inheritance, having been predestined according to His purpose who works all things after the counsel of His will, to the end that we who were the first to hope in Christ [Q] should be to the praise of His glory." "In Ephesians 1:11 it is used again and the purpose of it is explained in verse 12 by the infinitive, 'that we should be to the praise of his glory' (eis to einai), that is, 'For the purpose of being to the praise of his glory.'" (ibid

Endnotes, Appendix E

[Q] "We who were the first to hope in Christ" refers to the Jewish Christians, in contrast to the "you also" that follows in verse 13, which refers to the Gentile believers.

Copyright Permissions

Quotations from *The Complete Word Study New Testament* by Spiros Zodhiates, Th.D, Copyright © 1991 by Spiros Zodhiates. Used by permission of AMG Publishers, 6815 Shallowford Road, Chattanooga, TN 37421, USA.

Quotations from *The Challenge of Jesus* by N. T. Wright, Copyright © 1999 by N. T. Wright. Used by permission of InterVarsity Press, P.O. Box 1400, Downers Grove, IL 60515, USA. www.ivpress.com

Quotations from *Tyndale New Testament Commentaries, Colossians and Philemon* by N. T. Wright, Copyright © 1997 by N. T. Wright. Used by permission of InterVarsity Press, P.O. Box 1400, Downers Grove, IL 60515, USA. www.ivpress.com

Quotations from *The Normal Christian Life* by Watchman Nee, Copyright ©1957 by Angus I. Kinnear. 1966 printing, used by permission of CLC Publications. May not be further reproduced. All rights reserved.

Quotations from *What Shall This Man Do?* by Watchman Nee, Copyright © 1973 Angus I. Kinnear. 1973 printing, used by permission of CLC Publications. May not be further reproduced. All rights reserved.

Quotations from *Knowing God* by J. I. Packer, Copyright © 1973 by J. I. Packer. Used by permission of InterVarsity Press, P.O. Box 1400, Downers Grove, IL 60515, USA. www.ivpress.com

Quotations from *Lectures to My Students* by C.H. Spurgeon, Copyright © 1969. Used by permission of Zondervan. www.zondervan.com

Quotations from *The Purpose-Driven Life* by Rick Warren, Copyright © 2002 by Rick Warren. Used by permission of Zondervan. www.zondervan.com

Quotations from *25 Basic Bible Studies by Francis Shaeffer*, © 1987. Used by permission of Crossway, a publishing ministry of Good News Publishers, Wheaton, IL 60187, www.crossway.org

About the Author

Robert Harman has been teaching the Bible for over forty years and is passionate about seeing people established in their faith. He has taught this material in many places of the world, including Ukraine, Russia, Armenia, Nepal, Japan, Trinidad and Europe. It was previously published in Russian and 5000 copies distributed, but this is the first time it is available in English. A science major and graduate of William & Mary, he was a policeman for 26 years and a campus minister and pastor for 15. He and his wife, Johanna, live in Williamsburg, Virginia. They have two daughters and two adorable grandsons.

"My goal as you read is revelation — that God would speak to your heart and make His truth unshakeable in you."

I have created this book with you, the reader, in mind. From the beginning the lessons were created and used for a small group setting and nothing would please me more than to assist you in teaching these lessons to others. To that end, student notes are available, FREE, that you can download and print for your study group as 8.5 x 11 worksheets, and also other supplemental resources. Just visit my website, **RobertHarmanAuthor.com** for these and other free resources. You can also contact me there. I pray this book and the added resources will bring a rich, transformational experience in your pursuit of finding this hugely important 'one sure thing.'

Be truly blessed!
Robert

FREE DOWNLOAD

Student Notes

Get a free download of the complete set of Student Notes, study guides and extras at
RobertHarmanAuthor.com

Write the Author at:
Bob@RobertHarmanAuthor.com

Made in the USA
Middletown, DE
05 April 2023